HOUSEPARENTS IN CHILDREN'S INSTITUTIONS

A Discussion Guide

By

ALTON M. BROTEN

THE UNIVERSITY OF NORTH CAROLINA PRESS
CHAPEL HILL

Preface

The unsung heroes and heroines of our generations are those men and women who, without pomp and circumstance, without status or adequate return, give daily of themselves to tasks involving the upbringing of the youth of our land. To do so in ways that are truly helpful is an especial accomplishment.

High in the lists of such people are the men and women who work as *houseparents* in a great variety of child-caring institutions and similar group care programs across the nation. I am thinking particularly of those housefathers and housemothers (or counselors or child-care workers) who have been constant and caring and professional in their work with young children and adolescents for a significant period of time.

These houseparents are not too much interested in recognition from me or from others, although they want to feel that their work is important. They are much more interested in trying to understand the young people coming into their care and in having guidance in knowing how to use themselves and the tools at their disposal to meet the needs of these young people.

It is being said much more frequently and honestly today by professionally trained leaders in the residential group care field that we have become much more skilled in identifying the needs and problems of people, especially as individuals, without comparable insight into what it takes to help someone deal with these needs and problems, or to help a group to become a helping instrument in the lives of individual members.

The basic problems of a person may be difficult to reach and months and years of time may be involved. How can houseparents help youngsters to live day-by-day in ways which will be beneficial and have impact upon conflicts, fears, guilt, confusion, lacks, failures, patterns of behavior?

An experienced and successful houseparent knows that there can be no clear-cut, approved format for a particular residential program. What may be required depends so much upon the more specific purposes of the institution, upon the role that it is being asked to fulfill within its area of service. There can be no clear-cut, approved system of methods either for working with young people who are bewildered, disturbed, or homeless.

There are guides and guide-lines. However, every administrator and every houseparent must determine the specifics of how to work and how to help and how to work with individual problems and circumstances. Without giving up what is good and what works, there must be an ability on the part of these people to learn and to change. We have so much to learn together.

I have become convinced that houseparents and others who must throw themselves and all that they are into direct work with people, learn best through opportunities such as workshop-type meetings and discussions where they can think out loud with others about themselves, about what they do, about what they believe and sense, about best ways.

This booklet contains a number of discussion guides prepared, in most instances, with the help of houseparents in various institutions which I visited as a staff member of the Group Child Care Project from 1956 to 1961. They may well be used as the basis for a course of in-service training over six months, a year, or two years in a children's institution, and for this reason they are grouped into six groups of four, with two extra discussions provided to take care of times when there may be an extra session in a one-, two- or four-month period.

The "talks" which combine to form this booklet for houseparents were developed, for the most part, out of discussion groups which have been meeting, since 1956, on the campuses of some 30 child-caring institutions of six southeastern states: Virginia, North Carolina, South Carolina, Georgia, Alabama, and Florida. These institutions, affiliated with the Group Child Care Project (sponsored by the School of Social Work, University of North Carolina, and the Southeastern Child Care Association), have been part of a pioneer undertaking involving the use, on a regular basis, year after year, of two School of Social Work faculty members as "traveling teachers" or consultants. For a period of about four years, I carried the major responsibility for developing and meeting with these groups. As we began to know one another well, we were able to think together, very honestly, about many of the practical matters entailed in translating important goals and plans for children and youth into day-by-day group living. These "talks" reflect those deliberations.

Encouragement to assemble these chapters as well as help in editing and organizing the material has come from my former chief and colleague, Dr. Alan Keith-Lucas, Alumni Professor of Social Work and Director of the Group Child Care Project, University of North Carolina. His convictions about the potential of group-care and of the houseparent role are well known. I am proud to have had his help in planning this publication.

ALTON M. BROTEN

Contents

V. CHILDREN IN GROUPS

VI. ACTIVITIES AND OTHER PROBLEMS

VII. EXTRA SESSIONS

HOUSEPARENTS IN CHILDREN'S INSTITUTIONS

I. The Houseparent and the Job

1. A NOTE TO THE NEW WORKER

As a new staff member, you will feel that you are on "probation" with other staff members as well as with children. Most of them have been in the organization for a long enough period to feel settled. Yet each one of them has been new too. They may not always remember that. It is human to forget easily. You will find that most of them are willing to help you in various ways, once they are convinced of your earnestness, your honesty, your desire to learn and to be accepted.

Other staff members can be of help to you as you learn your way around. They can reassure you. They can give you very practical bits of information. You should, however, depend for the most part upon the director and supervisor for counsel, guidance and support.

An effort will be made to orient you gradually to your new responsibility. It may happen that, because of a critical shortage of staff, you must step right in and take over. It is usually best to carry through, at first, with the established routine and approach that has been followed; to be friendly but firm in proceeding along these lines; to be honest about having to learn but still to hold as much as possible to the program that has been recommended.

Children are often uncertain about a new staff member, no matter how fine a person she may be. "What will she change?" "Will she like me?" Although children may sometimes seem to provoke change, they do not like to see basic changes. It takes a while for them to accept the new. They may withdraw at first; they may adopt an aggressive attitude in order to find out what a new houseparent or dietitian will do; they may make many requests and demands as a way of testing out the new situation. As you are confronted with these experiences, you may want to say, "For now, we will do it this way. I will discuss your request with the director tomorrow and see what we should do"

When you first take over a group, you should know as many of the specific rules and procedures as possible—those that will come up, most likely, during the early days on the job. Hours, permissions, work schedules, medical appointments, study arrangements are among the points of information which you will need immediately. Later on, you will want other information of a more long-range significance. The more informed you are, the more sure you will feel in your job.

Most new workers feel uncomfortable with a group of children at first, no matter how much they like children. As you get to know them better and as they have an opportunity to know you, as you work through experiences with them, you will gradually grow in self-confidence and in assurance. Do a great deal of listening at first without prodding or pushing or interpreting.

Who are these children? In a majority of their needs, they are like any other children of their age. They are growing physically and intellectually. They have spiritual needs. They want to be liked and accepted. They want to succeed, to have fun, to make a contribution, to feel comfortable and cared for. They want to have persons and things "of their very own."

In certain ways, these children have special problems, not necessarily reflected at this time in the way they respond and the way they behave. Their problems are, for the most part, tied up with difficulties, out of the ordinary, which have confronted and upset the family circle to the point of separating family members, breaking up the home, creating an uncertain future, raising the possibility of conflicts towards adults and other children.

Most of the children come from homes which are physically broken. Parents are living but divided by divorce, separation, mental illness, physical illness, incarceration of one parent. The majority of these parents retain legal rights and probably could remove their children from care if they so desired. In some situations, the court is involved and must approve any change in plans. Most of these children have a parent or relative who is in varying degrees interested, who will visit and will have the children come for visits. Some parents can pay part of the cost of care.

A bond exists between these parents and their children. Even where there has been little experience of love, a special significance rests upon their relationship. The parent is part of the child's identity. What parents do and are and stand for reflects upon their children. Most children fear being abandoned by their "people" and long to return "home." They defend their parents against attack and choose to be loyal to the parent when a decision is pressed. To give up the parent seems to mean giving up part of oneself.

Many parents can be helped eventually to carry full parental responsibility once again. Many can be helped to carry part of this responsibility in collaboration with the agency. Some can never take on this responsibility and really want to be free of the children.

In the final analysis, we want the child to come to recognize what is true for him in his life. We want him to find out and decide what he can depend upon. He needs to learn to accept, to forgive, to understand, to be relieved, to see issues clearly. We do not help a youngster grow in this way by telling him what we think of his people, by passing judgments on parents—judgments which we have privately made to ourselves. If the houseparent is clear in what she stands for and assumes a non-judgmental approach toward parents and families, the child can be free to decide about his own people. The caseworker and the superintendent may be in a position to deal with these issues more directly than the houseparent.

Many parents will fail, have failed, or are "unfit" to care for their children. Yet we cannot draw a curtain in front of what has happened. The child's thoughts about his past still exist. His preoccupation with his family is still real and part of him. You may need the help of the caseworker in understanding how to work with a child who is seriously disturbed in this way.

Children will visit at home—in homes to which they may never be able to return on a permanent basis. When they return to the institution, they may be upset. You may bear the brunt of their feelings. They may sense that it is safer to sound off to you than to their parents, of whom they have so little and may be in danger of losing all. It is better, however, that children, except in extreme situations, are faced with the home situation as it is, rather than to live in a make-believe world. It is better for a child to face the truth gradually rather than to postpone the day of reckoning.

If you are like the majority of other new employees, you have entered this kind of work because you want to be able to associate with children who need you and who will accept your influence and guidance. It will not be long before you start to question the meaning of your position, your influence, your suitability and the attitudes of the children. You may find here something you had not counted on or do not seem fully to comprehend.

Boys and girls behave differently in groups than as individuals. Adults also are responsive to the influence of the group in which they find themselves or of the group to which they want to belong. What happens to individuals through group interaction can have tremendous constructive value for them. We try, in our work, to explore the possibilities which exist within group relationships and activities and to capitalize on them. Many of the boys and girls coming into care are going to be helped largely by what happens to them through living in groups.

Our primary interest is in the child and his family. In many ways, however, we work through group situations and relationships in order to help the individuals. For example, by assisting a group of youngsters to share work responsibilities in a cottage, we may help a child to feel that he belongs, that he has made a contribution of his own effort to the welfare of others, that he has done something for himself, that he is meeting society's expectations.

Many will benefit from the group relationships, the organization and routine of a cottage, the relationship with a houseparent. As you work along, you will, with other staff members, want to study the ingredients of cottage and group living and see what you can do to improve the quality of experiences available. We all have much to learn about the care of children in groups. This is not family living in a real sense, although we attempt to make cottage life as homelike as possible.

There will, of course, also be many opportunities for direct work with individual children. Other staff members such as the caseworker and the chaplain are available for special kinds of help.

As you develop as a staff member, you will become more and more skilled in group leadership. Always remember, however, that the individual's needs are the focus of the service and you will want to keep each child in mind, as much as possible, as you plan and work with your cottage group.

The cottage is where a child has his "own place." Here he has his belongings, his bed, his headquarters. Most of his permissions he secures from the houseparent of his cottage. It is important that he be happy and contented here, and it is toward this goal that we must work. The cottage must be a place in which its "residents" can relax and be themselves. They must feel that they can come to the cottage, that they have a right to be there, and that their interests will be protected and their needs considered.

We do not want the children to feel too different from other children. For this reason, we should attempt to create a home-like atmosphere within the residential unit. This means that furniture is comfortable and in good repair, that surroundings are appealing and attractive, that there is time and place to relax and be oneself (while showing proper regard for others).

If you are a houseparent, you will be expected to live with children much as a parent might *without* the full responsibilities of parents. You will have to be willing to settle down with them, to enjoy many of the things that they enjoy, to look after their physical needs day after day, to be available to them at night-time as the need arises. You cannot draw any one child to yourself as your very own, as a favorite. You cannot, no matter what your feelings might be, so involve yourself with any one child that you move into the parent's position completely. Some of these children might like to have all this attention. They may really need and want someone. Some may need a full-time parent, but could not live with one because of confused feelings. Your value as a houseparent is in relation to many children over a continuing period of time. It is not to only one child, now.

Each child is treated best when treated according to his own needs. In a group and especially with young children or more disturbed children, you will have to do the same (to a greater extent than in other situations) for one child as you would do for others. There still are ways, however, of varying your approach so that you meet personal needs. You will learn how to show your affection and concern for each child.

2. DIFFERENCES AND SIMILARITIES

Can the children's home or center be a substitute home? Can the houseparent be a complete parent to a "placed" child? Is it true that if boys and girls are cared for in the institution just as they might be in good private family homes, their needs and requirements will be most surely met?

What is a good home? Physical care is provided, few questions asked. There are usually two parents living, both of whom accept the responsibilities and the roles that are theirs. They live according to their deepest convictions and transmit their assurances, their beliefs to the children. A sense of loyalty exists between family members, in spite of minor disagreements. Activities are shared. There is chance for privacy. The pattern of daily living is consistent but not very routinized. Neighbors are not affected particularly by the conduct of the home. Children have the opportunity for the undivided attention of parents once in a while. The parents talk together. The family supports one another in the presence of others. The home provides some comfort. Each family member assumes a right and has a desire to have friends visit and be with the family. Each shares some responsibility for personal care and upkeep of home. There are innumerable opportunities for running errands, shopping, visiting in the neighborhood. The family plans together on important matters. Special permissions and arrangements can rather easily be made when desirable. Privileges are given according to age. Parents place more confidence in older children, base this on trust built through the years. As new ones are born into the family, care is taken to guide others so that they understand and accept newcomers. When rebuffed outside the household, a youngster has recourse and appeal to his own family. Each person feels a right to the home and many of its provisions; he knows he is there because he is wanted. With natural misgivings, parents help older children to grow up and away from home, always with the assurance they may return and share what the family has. When mistakes are made, parents stand ready to aid. Close relationships exist between parents and children. About the home, there is a comfortableness, an ease of movement, an openness. Attempts are made to do what is best for each individual.

Life in a children's home bears some similarities to the good home but also shows some striking differences. For some children, the institution may offer much more of the characteristics of a home than did their own homes. But the institution structure presents limitations in this respect. It possesses characteristics of its own, many of which can be used to the benefit of young people and families. To determine the special nature of the institution, let's look at some of the ways in which it and its people are different, are like others:

How are institution children different? They know that they are not living in their own homes, thus do not have the same rights. They are here because of special circumstances in their lives. These may have caused a break-up in the structure of their own homes; this may require that they defend themselves from criticism. If they have family members living, they have thought concerning their whereabouts, health, activity, interest, responsibility, attitude, promises; when the parent does not write, the youngster may wonder why and may blame himself for this failure. Confidence in self and optimism for future may be shaken by mysteries which have befallen the family; "Will the same thing happen to me?" There is no assurance that the future is secure. The institution does evict some children; parents occasionally demand their children. These young people are not always able to express their anger directly to their parents, so divert this to the persons close at hand; they feel some conflict in loyalties between parents and those taking care of them. Patterns of behavior which have been built up prior to placement continue to be followed even though the causes have to some extent been removed. Children may bring special problems with them, such as distrust of adults, difficulty in academic achievement, negative attitude toward religion, failure to succeed, excessive competition, fear of punishment or of being hurt, confusion as to role of adults.

How are they like other children? They seek companionship of other children, mostly of their own age group. They respond to the adult who shows a personal interest in them and a genuine understanding of them. They have need for daily activities. They seek to have the same privileges and personal attention that may come in a home setting. They want to achieve in something, and appreciate recognition. They need opportunities and privileges according to age and maturity. They require the normal limits and controls. They wish to be accepted and to belong. They want to be stimulated and to have things to do, to find privacy at times, to find adults in whom to confide and with whom to spend time.

How are their daily lives different? They are exposed to a routine which is less flexible. Work is assigned on a more arbitrary basis. Freedom in getting snacks and treats is limited. It is not possible for them to move as easily on and off campus and back and forth between groups on the campus. Dating opportunities are more restrictive and call for more "red tape." Group punishment is more often administered. The institution child is more conscious of how other children view his associations with adults. Personal contact between houseparent and child is more limited than between parent and child. There are more changes—new staff, new children, new rules, new activities. There is more pressure to meet deadlines. More children of the same age group live close together. They frequently are assigned work away from their own dwelling place. Mealtimes are on a larger scale and offer less chance for family-type discussions.

How are their daily lives like those of other children? They carry normal responsibilities in relation to school, to helping around the house, to getting permission from the adult living with them. They generally have their own beds, dressers, clothing and personal belongings. They have a fairly consistent bedtime hour. Provisions are made for their comfort and entertainment. They attend school and community functions relating to their age group.

How do houseparents differ from parents? They are salaried employees. They have not been with these children since birth, nor are they related to them. When the going gets too difficult, they are free to resign; they may be released. They have responsibility for a group of children, usually not related to one another. They do not carry any continuing legal rights or responsibilities in relation to individual children under care. The children are not a reflection upon the houseparent's family name. Regular time off and vacations, without the children, are planned. They usually do not carry the wide range of responsibility, such as for nursing the sick child, planning for special visits and the future, financing clothing needs, preparing meals, doing the laundry.

How are they like parents? Hours of work are long and not easily scheduled. They have responsibility for knowing where children are at all times. To be effective, they must live on an informal basis with children and not hold to strict relationships. They get across important lessons through the process of daily experiences. They must offer each child opportunity for personal, undivided attention. They are concerned when others criticize their children. They must recognize and allow for normal behavior, which is part of growing up. They cannot exist just for the satisfactions that they will receive from children. It is necessary that they have other adults with whom to

associate. They must support and encourage youngsters in their
dealings with others.

Other ways in which the institution differs from a home. Children
can be moved from one cottage to another, changing the identity of
the houseparent. Children do not always live with brothers or sisters;
seldom do boys and girls share the same cottage. The institution is
arranged on a larger scale with permanent business arrangements,
operates on a budget approved by others, and is supported by many
persons not personally known to the children. Activities can be affected by visitors and supporters who want to observe. It is hard to
show a connection between what is given and where it comes from.
By leaving the institution, the child usually loses his place there.
Children are expected to abide by regulations applying to many
others, even those outside the group in which they reside. The institution is not completely integrated into community life. It is set
apart, has a special name and a special reputation.

What does this all tell us? The institution contains special ingredients making it a valuable place for some children for a certain
length of time. It is not intended to be a good place for all who need
care away from home. Staff should strive to make it more homelike
but to realize that it cannot and perhaps should not be a complete
home for children. Our goals are not to have children conform in
order that they may be adjusted to the institution forever, but rather
that they adjust so they can gain help and preparation for resuming
life in the normal community. Staff members need consistently to
test the progress of individual children and work on plans for them,
within the institution program and in relation to future arrangements.
This cannot always be accomplished, but we should not be content
to sit back and let time, for the child, slip by.

3.   THE HOUSEPARENT CANNOT STAND ALONE

To some, the houseparent is the "hub of the wheel." Others
look to her as the person who, in the daily program, carries out the
treatment plan for each child. She is seen as a substitute mother
and a group leader. Whatever she is called, it is certain that the
houseparent's function is a most important one. She is different in
many respects from a mother in her own home. She differs also
from a group leader in a neighborhood house. The houseparent
finds that she cannot be satisfied with just keeping her cottage on an
even keel. The youngsters under her care relate to others and need
to have these opportunities. The houseparent herself needs help
from the rest of the staff, from persons in the community. She needs
other adults.

Why can't the houseparent go it alone?

Almost every child in the cottage is involved in some significant way with others outside the cottage and even outside the institution.

Each child has a future which must be planned for, entailing extensive and complicated work with family members, other agencies.

Each one has special needs that cannot be readily met within the framework of the cottage or by the houseparent.

Some children are not going to respond well to their own houseparent and may need association with other adults.

Problems and behavior of young people may require interpretation or special handling by others.

Young people in placement away from their own homes and families often need reassurance, assistance, and interpretation in relation to this separation.

To make certain that the institution does its part in helping parents to carry responsibility and make decisions and have meaning to children, it is necessary that continuing relationships be maintained.

Children in placement may need skilled help and guidance in feeling free and able to go along with the program, to learn from it and to participate in it. Often, this help must come from someone other than the houseparent.

Most youngsters have to have, in addition to good experiences in cottage living, opportunities for associating in a variety of ways with other children of their own age or sex, or of other ages and of the opposite sex.

Protection and controls over and beyond what a houseparent can provide may be essential for some youngsters because of their own problems or those of other family members.

With some young people who have complicated problems, the responsibility of daily care may be too much for one person to carry alone.

For her own emotional health and professional growth and development, it is necessary that the houseparent be able to turn to someone in a supervisory, helping capacity.

Children will move from the cottage and from the institution. It would not be good for the houseparent to try to be all things to her children, so that they could not readily form other attachments.

The stresses of the job of living steadily with youngsters coming from different backgrounds and presenting varied behavior make it mandatory that a houseparent periodically free herself from her work and take days off and vacation time. This requires that others be able to assume responsibility temporarily for the children.

Upkeep and maintenance of the cottage and surroundings require time and skill and expense, which the houseparent is not in any position to provide.

Planned programs of activities and events and opportunities are essential to the education, training, and enjoyment of young people and usually cannot be carried out by the houseparent, even though she may have ability along these lines.

The houseparent may find herself confused or upset or misunderstood in relation to institution procedure or other staff.

Youngsters frequently see special opportunities, such as for dating and outings and visits, that may involve others and be affected by public relations, policy, and procedure.

Some may, for a temporary period, require special care or treatment, at the institution or away from it.

Who and what does the houseparent need outside the cottage?

Someone, in a position of more responsibility, who can be available to help when the houseparent's own efforts in handling a situation fail.

Opportunities to confer on a regular basis with a supervisor, to talk over experiences, to see issues more clearly, and to realize alternatives.

Opportunities to meet together in group sessions, regularly, with other staff persons who are doing much the same job, to talk about matters of common concern.

Chances to join together with the total staff to discuss issues of general interest and to strengthen the bond that exists between all of these persons, to develop a smoother working program.

Opportunities to be a participant in case conferences, in which individual children are discussed in relation to their total experience and all their relationships, with a view toward coming to common understanding regarding needs and plans.

Someone, preferably a trained caseworker, with whom to share information and ideas and observations pertaining to the individual child and his family and from whom to gain assistance in understanding.

Chances for training and development, on and off the job.

Someone to take over responsibilities when the houseparent has time off and to do so in ways that will be constructive to the on-going life of the youngster in the institution.

Some adults to share in the practical program of providing for daily physical care of children, such as in areas of clothing repair, laundry, food preparation and serving, upkeep and maintenance of buildings, medical and dental care, extra cleaning.

Staff to work closely and continuously with the parent and also, individually, with the child, toward mutual planning and understanding, to clarify issues that arise, to plan for vacations and the future and to determine basic needs.

Someone in the field of recreation and activities to develop sufficient opportunities for leisure time activities and experiences, both on the institution campus and off the campus and to bring about such a program after careful consideration and understanding of the needs of individual children, the practical procedure of campus operation, and the responsibilities of the houseparent.

Staff to be concerned with helping individual children with special problems of finding their way, such as in education, in group activities, in work.

Some adults to help to develop, especially for older children, opportunities for more responsible and appropriate work activities and to be interested sufficiently so that they participate with the young persons in these experiences.

Special relationships for children who are very disturbed emotionally and require skilled help in finding their way through a mesh of personal problems and conflicts.

Whose work is most important? It would be impossible to say. Each staff member coming in direct contact with a child has to be informed, able, and ready to see himself as an integral part of the total. The houseparent has a big responsibility in establishing a pattern of daily life which can be beneficial to most of the boys or girls who reside in the cottage. Nevertheless, she has to see herself as part of the total program and only then will she be acting in the best interests of the young people. If a boy or girl finds satisfaction in the cottage, he or she may be strengthened or supported enough to gain additional values from other aspects of the program.

The houseparent, though she comes with sound experience and good personality, is not endowed naturally with the ability to find her way alone. She needs to learn with others and feel a partnership with them.

The houseparent and the teacher. So many "placed" children have, because of upsetting times in their lives, fallen behind in the educational program. What happens at home often is reflected in school and vice versa. This has been true before they came to the Home and will continue now, as well. It helps if the houseparent can know the teacher personally and have ways of transmitting routine information back and forth. Because of practical considerations, the case worker or some specially assigned person should work more closely and consistently with the teachers, providing them with fuller information and support and sharing with them ideas concerning how best to guide the children. Usually, the houseparent should work through this staff person except in the day-by-day arrangements that may be required. Opportunities for the houseparent to visit the school and see the work of the student, opportunities for the teacher to visit the cottage and the institution and see the living arrangements, the activity areas in which the child spends much of his time, all help to create better understanding between these important persons and demonstrate to the child himself that these adult people are willing and able to join ranks in serving him.

The houseparent and the caseworker. The caseworker has access to information concerning the child's life experiences and all his relationships; he has had personal contact with many members of the family, relatives, friends, and other interested persons and agencies. He has first-hand knowledge of the home surroundings from which the child has come and to which he is now related. He is maintaining a continuing relationship with the important persons in the child's life outside the institution. He carries a responsibility toward overall planning with parents and with the child and with other agencies. He has an awareness of the way in which all of the youngster's present experiences and relationships fit together. He has the ability to plan for private meetings with children and to talk over matters with them from the position of a person who is a staff member but who is not greatly involved in the day-by-day experiences. He has more freedom of movement in planning for trips, conferences, and visits enabling him to verify matters, obtain special help, participate in visiting by children and carry on working relationships with others in connection with the placement.

These characteristics of the caseworker's position will indicate his value and importance to the institution program, to the child and family, and to the houseparent. The houseparent may turn to the caseworker, not for help in deciding exactly what to do with her group in a given situation or what disciplinary action to take, but to get help in understanding the position of the child better, in clarifying issues pertaining to child and family, in guiding parents in their contacts with the daily care program, in assisting individual children to understand and accept and express feelings pertaining to daily experiences, in planning visits. The more that a houseparent understands of what the caseworker is doing with a family group and the more that the caseworker understands of what the houseparent is doing with the cottage group, the better chance there is that each person will carry his own responsibility in harmony with the job of the other.

The houseparent and the parent. The parents retain many very important rights in relation to their "placed" children, but give up, for the time being, rights in providing day-by-day care. Parents accept this fact in different ways. Some are able to be helpful. Others tend to undermine the placement. The houseparents and parents come into contact on visiting days, through correspondence, through phone calls. The houseparent should personally know who the parents are. She needs to be friendly and welcoming, but firm in relating to parents in connection with visits, contacts, and responsibilities. It is usually best that involved and complicated and continuing questions concerning rules and regulations, progress of children, plans for the future, health problems, feelings of the child toward placement and family, be referred to the caseworker or to the superintendent.

4. THE PERSONAL FACTOR

We have been perplexed by our inability at times to carry out in practice what we have conceived of as a good step, a good approach, a good technique. The trouble frequently may be that we have not reckoned with our own personal selves or the personality of the other person or persons.

Children come to live in group-care to have, as some say, "corrective experiences" in daily living. If we repeat what they have known before, we may become failures in helping them. If we can demonstrate as we live with these children good standards, attitudes and ways of meeting disappointment, and can combine this demonstration with a sincere interest in these same children, "corrective experiences" can often be realized.

To do this, it is essential that we be ourselves to a great extent. It is right that we should function in ways that are comfortable to us and are tied in with how we feel. Yet, there are times when, without losing our spontaneity, we must, in order to benefit others, withhold action, give support, offer suggestions, change a method, choose an activity, approach a problem in a way that we would not normally be inclined to make.

Parts of us that count. Various aspects of ourselves, our personalities, play into our ways of working with young people, and rightly so. As we think about who we are and what we are and how we look to others, we can gain an understanding that can assist us in meeting persons and situations. What becomes involved in our efforts to help others?

Appearance. What do I consider to be important? Of whom do I remind the person? Attitude that the person attaches to someone of my appearance.

Standards. What is important to me? How I consistently function. Relationship between what I preach and what I do.

Manner. Tie-up between this and what the child has known. Initial reaction. How a person sees me over a period of time.

Skills. Do I have some or do I lack most skills? The meaning of these skills to me. How do I transmit my knowledge, my interest?

Religious convictions. What do I really believe in terms of spiritual life, God, the life hereafter, the power of prayer, the relationship of doing good and being good?

Moral code. What seems especially important or significant to me? When do I become concerned, afraid, angry?

Frustration level. How quick am I to lose perspective, to lose my objectivity, to cease efforts to deal with a situation reasonably?

Give and take level. How much am I able to tolerate and understand? When do I see the need for taking action or for setting limits?

Personal concerns, worries. In what ways am I most vulnerable? Do I worry most about money, health, errors in judgment, or what?

Point of fatigue. What conditions cause me to reach this point? How much exposure? What do I do then?

Confidence, optimism. How do these characteristics of my general self show up? To what extent do I have these qualities? What seems to tear down or undermine them?

Usual reactions. To someone exercising authority. To danger. To weakness.

Prejudices. On sex, religion, wealth, poverty, appearance, authority, preachers, social workers, parents who have failed.

Goals and ambitions. What importance do I place on events, on actions that I take or do not take?

Defensive techniques. What ways do I have for dealing with personal difficulties, with problems I cannot handle? When does this have a direct or indirect bearing on my treatment of young people?

Ways of choosing friends. Can I make friends? What ways of making friends have I cultivated?

Fears, hates, loves, hopes.

Readiness to forgive. Can I really forgive? How do I show forgiveness?

What helps to determine the person I am? These characteristics may lend themselves to change or may not. Usually, recognition of them can lead us to an ability to use ourselves in the best possible ways in our dealings with others, especially those who come for help. These characteristics may have developed out of the following:

Experiences in growing up.
Experiences in adult life.
Job satisfaction.
Economic position.
Faith and religious experience.
Relationships with others, right now.
What we sense we have or do not have.
Physical strength and weakness.
Pressures upon us right now.

Education.

Chances we have had to rest and relax.

When the personal factor enters in. In group-care programs, we are confronted with innumerable situations which encourage us to draw heavily upon our own standards, prejudices, flexibility. These are some of the areas in which we might have to look at ourselves very closely:

The reception or acceptance of a newcomer.

Evaluation of language that a person is using.

Reaction to a child's attitude toward church-going.

Making allowances for a youngster who acts lazy, or does not try.

Living with a child who supports and defends a "no good" parent.

Counseling with someone who cannot learn, cannot grasp fundamentals.

Dealing with group antagonism toward authority, toward a rule.

Considering what to do about disobedience.

Helping youngsters to keep order, to do housework.

Guiding teen-agers in their dating.

Handling special problems, such as bed wetting and nail biting.

Working with other staff in reaching and supporting a group decision.

Co-existing with the other staff members.

Understanding the way in which a youngster accepts placement and the institution life.

We need to draw heavily upon our own experience, attitudes, and standards as we live and guide young people. But the pertinent questions must be, "Am I judging or acting or responding out of my own problems or limitations or am I trying to base my action upon what is going to be best and most helpful for the child? Can I look and reflect upon my own motivation and feelings in the matter? Can I be open to accept better solutions?"

II. The Child—His Past and Present

5. INFORMATION ABOUT CHILDREN

In some institutions, all information is shared with houseparents, to the extent of opening up the case records for reading. In others, little or no information is given. In many of our best institutions the goal is to provide each houseparent with that information which is essential for her work, which is important to her, or which she can use. This still leaves room for some difference of opinion as to the extent of frankness that surrounds the giving out of such information.

What do we mean by "background information?"
Reasons for placement.
Conditions presently surrounding the family; whereabouts; plans.
Child's experiences and relationships at home and in the community.
Facts concerning his previous school and church activity or lack of it.
Serious problems of family members. Their experiences.
Ways in which the family has lived. Standards. Training of children. Discipline. Care of clothing. Cleanliness. Manners. Associates.
Previous placements. Experiences and relationships in these settings.
Personality characteristics, mannerisms, habits, personal problems of child as demonstrated elsewhere. Bed wetting. Stealing. Fighting.
Persons other than family members who have been important to child. Neighbors. Playmates. Teachers. Camp counselors.

How and why this information is obtained. Usually this is obtained by a caseworker. His first purpose is to think with the family or with the agency about all aspects of the problems, to figure out what really is being asked, what really is needed. Caseworkers seek out only that personal information that is needed in order to arrive at a decision regarding the use of the institution or agency service. When it becomes apparent that placement is a likely plan, the caseworker then is in a position to seek additional information. Yet this is only that which can be of potential value to the agency in serving the child and family. These contacts by the caseworker are not limited to the gathering of facts, but take note of attitudes and feelings of the person or persons seeking help. Much of this may be important to the caseworker but not necessarily to others. Because these expressions are quite personal, they are dealt with in an atmosphere of confidentiality. The caseworker is charged with a responsibility to respect such information and to restrict its use as much as is good and practical, considering the welfare of child and family and considering the job to be done by the agency and its staff.

What does this information mean to the child? Generally, youngsters in group-care are not reluctant to reveal facts about their families and themselves to those whom they feel might and do understand, who will not be too quick or arbitrary in judgment and who will not discuss, indiscriminately and in general conversation, the personal facts they have revealed. Children in institutions—and to some extent in any home situation—want their rights protected in this regard. They do not want their parents or those who are substituting for their parents to talk about them and their families and their private home life. Young people, especially when in their teens, are very sensitive in this connection and may assume that two or three staff members talking together in private are talking about them, or that a conference called for some other reason is about them, or that casual comments by a school teacher relate to their personal lives. Some, for benefits to them which are not wholly desirable, may capitalize on a display of facts and feelings about their pasts. Some who are more settled, more confident, and more trusting may have come to the point where they can accept, to an extent, the interest of others in their personal lives. This entire area of information, however, must be approached by staff members with tact and understanding.

Houseparents, if they have information of a most personal and private nature, will want to discuss it with others on a professional basis. There is a place for this in most institutions. Such information should never be discussed publicly or on a conversational basis.

What is expected of the houseparent?

To work with a child in a total program which is attempting to relate his life now to the life which he has led and to the future.

To help the child to live with the problems he has or thinks he has.

To assist other staff members in getting at the cause of difficulty, in addition to dealing with symptomatic behavior. To join together in reaching a youngster. To draw in the help of others where needed.

To deal thoughtfully and considerately with parents and relatives who visit.

To prepare children for visits, for going away; also to help them with disappointments related to family, with re-adjusting after visits, with dealing with correspondence and phone calls.

It is a fact that:

Whether or not the houseparent is given information by the caseworker or administrator, she will come into possession of such information, from the child himself, from the parent who visits, from the relative, from correspondence which the child shares, from the last houseparent. Such information may not always be accurate. It may even be misleading.

Not all houseparents are prepared or able to handle information in the same way. They do not all have the same capacity for understanding, for acceptance, for confidentiality. Some may find it particularly hard to understand certain problems, such as mental illness of a parent. Some may be more inclined to judge children in relation to parents, or in relation to brothers or sisters.

There may be some who live in fear that staff members will find out the truth about them or their families. It might be better for them to know that houseparents know and still accept them and their parents.

Staff members generally use information more intelligently, professionally, and wisely, when they are given such information in a planned way by those who are in a position to know; when it is the basis for further discussion and planning for the child; when there is a method calling for all staff to be a part of this process of mutual understanding and planning.

The best results come when:

There is a staff-wide philosophy that each staff member dealing directly with a child is entitled to important information and especially to that which will help her, in her particular job, to work with the child intelligently. That each staff member is almost equally informed, though working in somewhat different ways.

Consistent interpretation and emphasis is made before the staff, through conferences and individual supervision, concerning the proper use of information.

There is a system of staff conferences in which children and families are discussed from the standpoint of determining current situation and progress and problems, of re-working tentative plans and deciding on new ones, of coming closer to understanding what is true, what is needed.

There is a philosophy of "sharing" of information between caseworker and the houseparent, rather than a one-way process, so that the houseparent is made aware of the existence of a channel for communication of this type of material.

The houseparent has an opportunity to be in on the plans even prior to admission and shares in the decision as to whether the child can be accepted or not.

Case records are kept as the property of the casework department and are not open to use by other staff or children. Much of this information has meaning primarily as a work record for the caseworker and administrator and must be interpreted to the staff.

Special attention is given to helping the staff member who has difficulty in understanding and accepting certain information. Limits are set to the extent to which information is given in the area which is a problem for this staff member.

Children in being admitted are reassured that the caseworker and the houseparent, especially, know the pertinent information as to why placement was necessary and the general conditions of the home.

6. OUR CHILDREN HAVE FAMILIES

Most of us recognize that the vast majority of boys and girls being cared for in institutions today are coming from broken homes not caused by the death of a parent. In most cases, both parents are living. Frequently, one or both parents have remarried. With our increased use of other resources, we may find too that families are split in placement, with some children in one institution or boarding home and others in another. Most of us would agree, in words at least, that, in giving services to a child, we must consider him in relation to his total family. Most of us do not question the wisdom of working with the cooperative, more responsible parent. But this assignment is not an easy one for us. To embrace the entire family in our sights causes us to consider many more lives, many more factors and issues.

Some of the things we say and believe:

Parents have rights and responsibilities toward their children, under the law, until such time as the court clearly reassigns these rights and responsibilities. This reassignment should only be done when the parents have clearly demonstrated their inability or unwillingness to carry them. Properly, then, we need to show respect for these rights and responsibilities of parents as we draw up and follow policies and procedures.

A significant, important psychological bond exists between parents and their children, regardless of their experiences together. We have to exercise great caution in dealing with this bond. It is not always based on love for one another. Pride and affection for family members are inestimable values for a child's growth. We ought not to tear down without putting something in its place.

We can understand reasons for the parent's dilemma, for the need for placement of the children. Participation in arrangements for placement may be sound and wise on the parent's part. Although the parent carries responsibility for his own actions, there are powerful influences rising out of the practical situation faced and the experiences of the past that help to determine these actions.

Most parents, as is true of any other persons, can learn, progress, mature, change under the right stimulation, when encouraged and helped by someone who strikes a responsive chord. Many need only support and an easing of their burdens. Others need special and skilled help. Some can learn through observing those who care for their children. Because of a series of discouragements, some parents need to be "courted" in order to make beginning steps.

In providing care to children away from their own homes, it is generally beneficial to encourage parents in consistently showing interest, taking some responsibility, participating in planning, testing out their own abilities. As children grow older, it helps to consider with them aspects of their family relationships and experiences. Fantasies and idealization of parents occur most frequently when the parent is left out or chooses to be left out without the child knowing what is happening.

Institution programs are in a unique position to be of service to both children and their families. Certain inherent conflicts are not present here (if the staff is conscientious) that may be present in foster family care. We can give parents chances to demonstrate what they can do, to test out their ability to become parents again. We can arrive at decisions with them which will eventually lead to more permanent planning for their children. This may result in their becoming "complete" parents, "partial" parents, or in their giving up their rights and responsibilities.

If we agree with all these points, in principle, we are faced with other questions that emerge in carrying out a program that includes the parent and family.

What can we do when the family situation has disintegrated too far by the time that it comes to us?

When distance or staff shortage are factors, what substitute arrangements can be effective for working with families?

How can we give a child a "corrective living experience" when his family will not let him alone to use the experience, or when his visits or other contacts with his family are too upsetting and prevent his settling down?

What do we do when there is conflict between the child's welfare and the parent's welfare?

How can we work with parents who are imprisoned or hospitalized?

We cannot get involved in all the intricate problems of some families. Where do we stop?

When do we seek legal action to protect the child? When do we seek legal action to terminate parent's rights?

How can we work with the very disturbed or the very immature parent?

Does "work with parents and families" necessitate the services of a specialist?

How can we think of rehabilitating a home that has never been a home, where family members have no concept of the climate needed for a decent home?

Should we allow parents the privilege of having us care for their children while they are young—and then of demanding them back home when they are older and able to work and add to the family's income?

There are many ways by which "work with parents and families" can be carried out. It might involve the caseworker's interviews with the parent. It might entail the experiences the parent has in working with and participating with the institution staff in caring for the child. It could be through the parent's contacts with a supportive, authority-carrying person. The parent might get most of the help needed through just having the child cared for while he works out other important plans. The parent might be helped through confronting a law or policy or procedure.

Looking more closely, these are among the possibilities for working with parents:

Through the actual service of the agency:

Protection, limits, control for the child.

Financial assistance. Sharing of the financial burden.

Good physical health care for the child.

Relief from caring for the child; freedom of time for work.

Through relationships with the program:

Observation of what good care means and what it costs.

Understanding of what the community expects, demands.

Recognition of the kindness and consideration of others.

Experience in meeting requirements and expectations; keeping rules, regulations.

Sense of support and participation of others in care of children, in solving family problems.

Experience in planning for children, taking responsibility.

Knowledge of what child needs, likes to do, can do.

Identification with the control, protection, security gained by the child.

Relief of personal pressures.

Experience in communicating with others.

Experience in accepting the interest of others in one's children.

Sense of pride, of personal worth, of dignity in dealing with staff.

Recognition of child's worth in being accepted by others.

Experience in controlling and limiting own impulses and urges.

Through relationship with the caseworker or other agency representative:

Insight into child's needs and what has been happening to him.

Beginning insight into one's own needs, problems, failures and strengths.

Discovery of someone in whom to trust, on whom to depend and whom one can test out.

Figuring out what responsibility one can carry, and clarifying legal responsibility.

Facing facts realistically, to see what can be done.

Starting work toward future arrangements.

Expressing one's own ideas and feelings about the program, about being helped.

A sense of the earnest support and interest of another.

Learning what alternatives and resources are available.

Understanding why the agency must work the way it does.

Learning the nature of the parent-child relationship and how to communicate within it.

Sensing one's own feeling toward one's child.

Demonstrating concern for the care of the child.

A crucial time in our work with families is the time prior to and including admission of a child into care. During the pre-admission period our organization sets the tone for future relationships with the child and with the family. We seek out the family ourselves where possible to arrive at agreements and understandings.

It is difficult to think of a child's welfare without also thinking of the family's welfare. This does not mean we always think of the rehabilitation of the original home and family group as being practical and best. Experience has taught us that we cannot and should not separate our considerations of the child from that of family. Experience has taught us, too, that when we have been conscientious throughout in our consideration of the total family, our results have been more rewarding.

7. QUESTIONS WHICH LEAD TO UNDERSTANDING A CHILD

We cannot understand anyone by a single characteristic, but rather must look at the whole child and see him in relation to what we know of normal personality development, and to what we know of him as a unique person. The questions which follow may encourage you to look more objectively at the child and his problems and also at your own relationship to the child. Through this, you may be in a better position to see what help the child really needs from you or from others.

How does the child present himself?

What is his school standing—in terms of placement, grades, achievement, aptitude, incentive, relationships to teachers and pupils?

How does he get along with other children in the cottage?

How does he respond to the houseparent and to other adults on the campus?

Are his actions appropriate to his age group or to his sex?

In what ways do his physical characteristics affect his behavior?

Does he have particular talents or interests?

What relationships does he have or seek with members of his own family? What are his attitudes toward them? How does he react to visits or non-visits?

How does the child respond to the other adults or children outside of the institution or family?

Does he form close attachments to others? Is this done easily? Do they last?

Is he subject to moodiness? What is the intensity, length, and immediate cause of these moods?

Are tantrums part of his makeup? When do they come? How long do they last? What effect do they have?

Does he show nervous mannerisms, such as tics, nail biting? Is he a bed-wetter?

What is his facial expression? Does he laugh at or with others? At what does he laugh?

Does he appear to express his true feelings in an appropriate way? In what does he excel?

Does he respond to encouragement and praise? In what way?

Does he show a willingness to participate or to help himself? Determination? Some personal goals?

What does he show in the way of reaction to his placement?

Can he compete? In what way? To what extent?

How does he take responsibility? Does he help others? Does he volunteer or do only what he is asked?

Is he a leader, a follower, or an isolate in the group?

What do material things mean to him?

Does he show that he knows the difference between right and wrong?

Does he admit mistakes and try to correct them—or does he project blame on others?

How does he respond to personal attention and affection?

Does he show a confidence that his own needs will be met or does he feel he will be short-changed and must therefore be first and get the most and best for himself?

How does he react to limits, to correction, to punishment?

Does he show respect?   In what way?

Does he appear to have cycles of behavior?   What seems to set these off?

Will he stand up for his own rights?

What are his attitudes toward spiritual matters?   Toward the religious program?

What does he do with his free time?   To what extent does he try to be by himself?

What lies behind the child's behavior?

Is he large or small for his age and how does he accept any difference?

What is his I.Q. and how is this reflected in behavior or work?

Is his school placement right for him?   Does he find any sense of achievement there?

Do we have him with the right cottage group or with the right roommate?

What does the houseparent mean to him, and what does he mean to the houseparent?

What have been his past experiences and environment, and how might these color his present adjustment?

What heredity factors affect his life?

What is the status of his family and how does this affect him? Have there been changes in the marital status of his parents?

What contacts does he have with his family and what do these persons mean to him?

Does he have someone to cling to as an ideal?

Does he have goals or hopes for the future?

Has he had opportunity to visit with family or to visit "back home"?

Under what conditions was he placed?   What is his acceptance of the institution?

How long has he lived at the institution?

At what age did he have to leave his mother or mother-substitute?

Has he had opportunities to decide for himself or to make choices?

Does he have anything in which he can excel or take a personal interest?

Does the institution provide him with sufficient opportunities to develop own interests?

Is there space for privacy in his cottage?

Am I judging him on the basis of his past mistakes only or on the basis of his brothers' or sisters' adjustment?

Has some adult proved to him that he is really cared for?

What is his parents' relationship to the institution?

Has the staff shown respect for his parents? For him?

Does he feel he can confide in a staff member even when he has done something wrong?

Does he have the impression that adults can set and hold good limits for him?

Do I expect more of the child than his age, intelligence, or maturity permit?

As he reacts to his problems, does he tend to withdraw or to act out impulsively?

Has he known bitter disappointment or shock?

As we more thoroughly understand each child with whom we work, we know that our approach to each one will be, to an extent, different. We can be flexible within the institution framework. Every child who comes to us has many special needs of his own. To accept him into our care means that we will try to help him answer those needs.

8.   THINGS WHICH CANNOT BE CHANGED

We would all like to remove from the shoulders of children the worries and conflicts, the difficulty and unsettling experiences of the past, the limitations that they have, so that all would be well again with them and they would be able to face the future with a great amount of hope and security. Unfortunately, we are unable to resolve, or change, or erase everything that perplexes or handicaps a child. Frequently we, as helpers, must recognize the necessity of assisting others in living with much that cannot be changed. In group-care, how do we do that? Even where efforts are being made to reach into the depths and permit children to see more clearly, to understand, and to correct, it may be necessary now to help those same children to live for a long period with things as they are. The act of living with experiences of the past may be part of the process of healing.

Things which resist change or erasure:
The fact of illegitimate birth.
Mental illness of a parent.
Observation of violence at home.
The fact of death of a parent through suicide.
Desertion by the parent.
Mental deficiency in the family.
Limitations of physique or coordination.
Unpopular traits.
Effeminacy, tomboyishness.
The fact of having hurt someone else.
Adoptive status.
Lack of interest on part of relatives.
No home to which a visit can be made.

How can a person best deal with these?

Come to recognize one's own responsibility and one's own error, but not carry guilt which is too heavy or misplaced.

In spite of difficulties, not feel too different from others.

Recognize realistically what has happened or what the situation is. Begin to see why's and wherefore's.

Not carry hatred or bitterness.   Forgive.

Not see misfortune as a specific punishment by God for a specific sin.   Recognize God's interest, concern, expectations.

Recognize bright spots, one's own strength and talents.   Have hope.

Begin to see what can be done to remedy, alleviate and overcome.

Experience the possibilities and satisfactions in relationships today.

How houseparents can help:

Show a respect and acceptance of the individual child.

Demonstrate acceptance, tolerance and understanding of child's "own people."

Give recognition to what a youngster can or could do well.

Avoid popular "type casting" of people, such as the mentally ill, jail-birds, deserters, alcoholics.

Avoid sharp inflexible judgments of other people which could lead children into greater conflicts regarding their own relatives.

Help create healthful, constructive relationships between children and between children and oneself and other adults.

Help children to develop their own talents and abilities.

Show a recognition of the differences in persons, yet a general attitude of fairness and respect for everyone.

Support and work with youngsters in arrangements to visit at home or in making plans.

Use caution in agreeing with children on snap judgments about their own relatives or homes.

Support children in their daily relationships to God and in their search for spiritual truths. Offer them regular experiences in these relationships.

Recognize who are the staff persons who can help children with particular issues and steer children to the appropriate persons.

Demonstrate a readiness to forgive.

Be ready to listen to what young people have to say about themselves, without being too hasty to "gloss over" or too quick to pass judgment.

Show a firmness in one's own convictions and purposes in life without imposing these on children.

Demonstrate a personal optimism about the future and a friendly and positive feeling toward the Home, other staff, and the children in general.

Offer to children as much as possible a genuine spirit of enjoyment, peace of mind, assurance and happiness. Laughter and fun and pleasant associations with others have a tremendous influence.

How other staff members help:

Where a child meets fairly consistent acceptance and understanding by many adults, the help that he needs will come to him more rapidly. These repetitive experiences will tell him, more than anything else, that there is hope, that there is nothing to be afraid of and that there is value in him. The caseworker, the teacher, the minister, the nurse, or the superintendent may be in a better position than the houseparent to point out and clarify important issues about special problems. The youngster then may return to his cottage to work out his thoughts and pattern for actions. There are those on the staff, such as the houseparent supervisor, who can point out to a houseparent what she is or is not doing to help. Together they can move toward better solutions.

III. Relationships with Children

9. HOW CLOSE SHOULD I GET?

Houseparents are supposed to be human, to be persons who can enjoy other human beings, to demonstrate a warmth and a responsiveness in relationships which is unquestioned and easy for young people to see, to be interested in more than just the routine and physical care and achievements of young people, to be concerned about a youngster's motivation and attitudes.

Often children behave as they do because of a lack of personal affection and attention. Many of them need to be physically close to those around them. They need to feel that others can come close to them and like being in their company. There are many who would like to have the houseparent all to themselves, even though their actions might seem to indicate the opposite. Some young people are quite ready to think of houseparents and other institution staff as parents. Others are much more cautious.

We wonder whether we ought to allow children to call us "Mom," "Pop," "Daddy," "Mommy." Further than that, we may wonder whether we should touch a child, either in affection or in punishment. Most persons who are "right" for continuing work with children are those who have a normal and natural need and inclination to live with children, to be in their physical company, to show feelings rather clearly, to touch a child when it seems best and necessary. But there are differences between them. Some show their affections more directly by putting their arms around children or by kissing them good night. Others demonstrate their affection more through the way they talk to children, do for them, walk with them, play or work with them.

Some of the goals of our work:

To indicate to a young person that we like him, respect him, want him in the cottage.

To indicate that others can enjoy being in his company.

To make it increasingly possible for him to trust in adults, to be honest and frank with them, to show himself as he really is.

To help him realize the humanness of others—so that he can better accept his own limitations.

To help him feel a consistency of care, to know what to expect, to feel assured that the affection shown by another will continue through "thick and thin."

To help him begin to sort out his feelings and information regarding his parents and family and come to resolutions concerning his status in relation to them and in relation to houseparents.

To give him some concept of the appropriate roles of father and mother in a family, and of man and woman. To see how they carry their responsibilities in relation to the children.

To help the young person feel assured of the affection of those around him and yet be able to make the move into the world or to another cottage.

This means for us:

That we have to try to show a respect and liking for every youngster who comes to live with us. When we react negatively to someone, we need to bring those feelings out in the open and discuss them with the supervisor, or with the caseworker who could give us further understanding of the child's position.

That our focus must not be on our own personal needs and satisfactions. It is all right and necessary for us to be human and natural in our approach to children, but we should not, for the sake of the child, try to take on the children as though they were our "very own." We ought to be clear that we cannot be a "full parent" to any child in our care. We ought not to confuse him or ourselves about it.

That we keep the lines of communication open, so that boys and girls can feel free to express themselves frankly in our presence. If they sense that we are competitive with their parents or that we are too judgmental about them, they may "clam up" and resist us. It is best to avoid any situation in which we pass judgment on the parent or offer ourselves in the place of the parent.

That we go "easy" in expecting affectionate response from children or in demonstrating our affection. This would particularly hold true for most older children, for those who have been starved for affection and those who question the meaning of outward displays of affection because of their previous experience with adults who have not loved them.

That we individualize our relationships depending upon the overall responsibility that is ours; that we figure out, in our daily programs of care, how we can best demonstrate our interest and liking and affection for every child in our care.

Specific guides:

Houseparents can seek an opportunity each day, if at all possible, to speak to each boy or girl in the cottage—if only for a brief period

—but alone if possible. This may be in a corridor, at study time, after school, in the morning. It need not be anything more than discussion about what has happened in school.

They can show understanding in how they show a youngster affection. It may involve a pat on the shoulder, a handshake, a kiss for a younger child, sitting next to a boy or girl at TV or study time, or the giving out of a treat or snack.

Doing something together is usually the best way of building close relationships. The houseparent who works along with young people as they do their assignments or who joins in their leisure time activity or who comes to school to observe their work or who helps them prepare a special treat in the kitchen will accomplish much more than the houseparent who remains aloof and reaches youngsters through individual counseling sessions in her room.

As children figure out our relationship to them, they may experiment with names and titles. They may copy other children. They may bestow on us titles normally reserved for parents or grandparents. They may choose first names or nicknames. Generally, the particular name is not as important as the meaning that goes with it. If the youngster calls the houseparent by the first name with the thought of looking upon this person as someone less than an adult, then this is unacceptable. If the child calls the houseparent "Mommy" or "Daddy" because of a definite desire to have this person take the exact place of their parent, then this may have to be reckoned with. The response of the staff member is equally important in determining whether a name or title is helpful or harmful. If the adult is clear in not wanting to replace the real parent or not wanting to be a playmate or a brother or sister of this child the title will be no more than a convenient and comfortable way of addressing the grownup.

The houseparent can periodically ask herself when she has a question about her approach with a child: "By my approach or relationship with this child, am I going to make it possible or extremely difficult for him to move on to another cottage or into his own home or a substitute family home?" The answer to this question may give her a clue to what she is doing.

It is a struggle to show some children any interest at all. Some are hard to like. Some make it hard for us to like them. The only way we can overcome this is through acquiring understanding of such a child and through finding ways of participating with him. There are those who would be confused by our personal interest in them if displayed too openly. There are some who, if stimulated by our interest, would make over-exaggerated demands for our time. With the help of the caseworker or supervisor, we may, through understanding, spot these young people and determine how best to work with them. We may have to wait for them to seek us out rather than too openly seeking to build close relationships with them.

Usually with younger children, we have little problem in getting a positive response to the interest we may show them. Houseparents cannot spend the time in individual activities that parents can, however, and the houseparent, to avoid over-giving one day and having nothing left over for the next day, may have to pace herself in her activity within the cottage.

Older children need adults as much but often do not show their feelings as openly. A successful houseparent with older children knows how to sense their affection without requiring an outward display of it. They like to be less obvious in their dependency relationships.

Finally houseparents cannot be "cold fish." Nor can they just open up their hearts and offer children their affection and love and expect an immediate return. Young people who have been bruised by experiences in their own homes as well as in the institution and former foster homes may not always respond in spontaneous ways.

10. THE SORT OF RELATIONSHIP THAT HELPS

Much of the work that a child-caring institution undertakes with children and their families is aimed at assisting these persons in finding solutions, in overcoming the impact of upsetting and disturbing experiences, in furthering a process that will help to heal bruises and cure emotional ills. Children who are placed often need to find ways of dealing with these problems:

Not feeling really loved.
Uncertainty about themselves, of their place, of care or protection.
Inability to express themselves honestly.
Being mixed up in loyalties.
Fear of growing up.
Inability to trust or depend upon adults.
Inability to see a hopeful future.
Not feeling worthy or entitled to rights.
Blaming oneself unreasonably.
Not knowing what is important, right and good.
Not being sure when to stop in terms of behavior.
Feeling misunderstood, mistreated.
Sensing bitterness toward people, toward life.

Placement in a group-care setting can bring into play, for the child, several factors which can help him, provided that the placement

has been arranged thoughtfully and responsibly and with consideration of family ties and rights.   Most significant and important are
the interpersonal relationships which the youngster has as an individual, or as a group-member, with his—

> Group-mates (other children).
> Houseparent.
> Caseworker.
> Group worker.
> Work supervisor.
> Recreation leader or coach.
> Nurse.
> Minister.   Chaplain.
> Superintendent.   Director.
> Teacher.

Through living day-by-day with these men and women, by re-
peated experiences that are strongly connected with reality, more
child-centered, more considerate of the rights of others, more struc-
tured to his own needs than elsewhere, and by gaining consistent
guidance and help in understanding himself and his situation, the boy
or girl placed in group-care should find clarification for puzzling
issues, satisfactions which will substitute for losses, security in knowing that care is provided, and assistance in understanding and in
working out plans.

To meet the many special needs of boys and girls placed away
from home, the child-caring institution must offer a wealth of possibilities for these interpersonal relationships that will help the healing
process.   These possibilities may be found within staff members or
within those who are in the community but are related to the institution's program.

In dealing with children and especially those who have great
needs, the adults cannot leave the responsibility for initiating relationships to the children alone.   There must be a reaching-out, a cultiva-
tion, an encouragement.

> *Ingredients of a helping relationship:*
> Personal interest.
> Recognition of the other's importance and dignity.   Respect.
> Experiences together.   Interaction of thoughts, interests, and
> action.
> Resiliency, flexibility, tolerance of ideas.   Readiness to under-
> stand.
> Compatibility.   Willingness to be close to the other person.
> Continuity of experiences together.

Stability, sense of security, firm standards, confidence, optimism of the helping person.

Awareness of and relatedness to reality.

Appropriateness to one's own role. (Adult acting as an adult.)

Confidential approach which recognizes honestly what must be shared.

What these points imply is that the helping adult—whether he be the houseparent, the teacher, the recreation leader—must be the right kind of person to begin with, must have an understanding of human beings and the many kinds of problems they may face, must have the ability to think of the other person and not himself, must be in a position which will allow him to help, must be able to move out and interact with the person needing help, and must have a good understanding of and dedication to the particular role that is his.

As children have influence upon one another, many of these factors may also apply in determining whether they will be of help to a newcomer, to a withdrawn child or to an acting-outer.

Avenues for building relationships. The teacher, caseworker, minister have their ways of building relationship. The houseparent works in certain ways which are closely identified with the responsibilities for day-to-day living. Through these experiences with children and young people, the houseparent can establish meaningful relationships:

Keeping house.

Helping with homework.

Showing interest in school experience.

Settling quarrels.

Placing children thoughtfully in regard to bedrooms, job assignments.

Encouraging participation in activities.

Helping to satisfy special interests.

Supporting a visiting plan.

Giving comfort after a disappointment.

Recognizing the effort of a child.

Serving, preparing appetizing food.

Talking to children about God. Participating in devotions.

Guiding children in relationships to others.

Handling bed-wetting, tantrums.

Dealing with special requests for dates, to go downtown.

Caring for clothes.

Enjoying games or cottage activities.

Setting or clarifying a rule.

What is most important, of course, is that which goes into these experiences in an on-going way. Sincerity, assurance, thoughtfulness, knowledge, timeliness—and many other intangibles—are the ingredients put into the experience by the houseparent and these tell the story.

11. LEARNING THROUGH LIVING TOGETHER

Houseparents, as well as parents, are engaged in teaching. Although they work much more informally than the classroom teacher, the challenges and broad goals are much the same. The teaching done by the houseparent is accomplished through experiences in living together with children. Ideas, information, standards, and attitudes are put across through these associations, in very subtle ways.

Successful teaching is possible only with those who have a reason and a willingness to learn. When this spirit is dampened, the effectiveness of education is also dampened. The willingness of boys and girls to learn from associations with others—adults and other children—is often related to how they feel in the situation, how they see the other persons and what they think of them.

Although the "teaching approach" must be blended into the way of living guided by the houseparent, it is important for her to be aware of what she is trying to get across and how this may best be done. Her methods, however, must not take away from her own warmth and charm.

What are we after?   To contribute to the growth and development of a "happy and responsible adult." While realizing that there are many variables which affect the kind of adult into which a child will grow, we nevertheless strive to help him develop some of these characteristics:

Ability to take responsibility both in personal relationships to the community and toward God.

Consideration and appreciation of other human beings.

Confidence in his own ability to grow and develop.

Ability to love.

Ability to tolerate a normal measure of frustration.

Knowledgeability about life and confidence in facing it.

Ability to be himself.

Readiness to make friends and confide in them.

Settledness in terms of own past experience. Generally has resolved any major conflicts.

Ability to enjoy himself with others and not at their expense.

Incentive and enough drive to decide, to act—yet an ability to relax and see what is most important in life.

Skillfulness in working and living with others.

A child therefore needs to learn that:

He will be cared for and protected according to his real needs.

There are people who can like and love him as he really is, with both his good and bad points.

He is important and unique in himself and has a place and rights.

God sees and cares for him as a person.

He carries certain responsibilities toward God, himself, and his fellows and, as he grows, will be more accountable for all that he does.

He has potential for growth, development, improvement.

He can be limited, corrected, and forgiven.

His family can be the source of his concern, consideration, understanding, and pride, even though they have made errors, been limited, had certain major weaknesses.

Others enjoy something about him.

He can gain satisfaction from doing for others.

He can admit to wrongdoings and errors without being hurt.

The future hold hope for him and others.

All the blame for what has happened does not rest on him.

He can say what is on his mind.

To "give in" or accept authority does not mean loss of self-esteem.

He can make choices and mistakes without tragic results.

Consequences come from certain actions and can be accepted without upheaval.

Other persons have opinions and skills, too, which are important.

Also, he should learn:

How a family lives together in a community.

What things cost.

The rights of other people.

Ways of mixing with others in truly satisfying ways.

Ways of pursuing individual interests in satisfying ways.

Rules and limits which govern all. Consequences of bad actions.

Best ways of taking care of his physical self.

How to judge persons one can trust.

How do young people learn? These lessons are learned best by young people from experiences with other persons, who, purposely or unintentionally, have a stake in the situation, are involved in it in some important ways. As we think of children in the institution, it is easy to see that they learn from different persons, such as:

Those who appeal to them or with whom they identify. These persons may include adults and other children.

Those who do not appeal to them but who are deeply involved or entangled in the situation.

Those who are in authority or control and who, thus, press ideas upon the child or the group. Again, these persons may be adults or other children.

What a child accepts or "catches" and makes part of himself may come more from the way in which an interpretation is put across than from what actually is stated or set forth. This, then, puts a higher priority on methods and attitudes of staff persons than on words or actions. The tone, the atmosphere, the climate, the manner play greater roles in this type of learning than we are often ready to admit.

Conditions under which better learning can take place:

The *situation* must be right:

The cottage group is of reasonable size and content.

An adult is in place of authority and able to exercise good controls.

Privileges and freedom are provided for according to age, maturity.

Opportunities are available for individual as well as group activity. There are chances for a young person to find privacy.

The group is generally a relaxed one.

There are no strong cliques which dominate the cottage.

There is a general feeling of "unity" within the group and a readiness to pull together.

There is no strong conflict between the group and others on the campus.

The cottage offers the same opportunities for each child to be accepted, to take responsibility, to be protected.

A certain framework including rules and methods of living together is simply and clearly prescribed and carried out.

No one child is in a position of dominating the group.

Attempts are made to encourage participation of each child and to provide variety in the cottage makeup and experiences.

The *houseparent* must be right:

Accepts most children—their looks, pasts, strengths and weaknesses.

At the same time, expects growth and progress from them.

Has ability to tolerate situations and characteristics without lowering his own standards and goals.

Combines firmness and kindness.

Combines honesty, sincerity, directness.

Has confidence in his own ability to manage and to enjoy the group.

Is able to understand language and thinking of the age group and to find common ground for conversing and working together, while still carrying responsibilities.

Adopts a consistent approach to children.

Is willing to listen and to find out what a child is really like and is really thinking.

Makes himself available; works along with youngsters.

Is generally relaxed; takes events in stride usually.

Is not too quick to judge.

Has ability to control, to punish—without losing equilibrium.

Practices what he preaches.

Acts in responsible ways toward group; does not openly converse with others about problems of group.

The *child* must be right:

Physically well.

Accepting of placement.

Not too much concerned or worried about his own people.

Not overwhelmed by guilt for things not within his own responsibility.

Unafraid of other children.

Assured of protection.

Assured of well-meaningness of most of the adults around.

Having some conviction of his own worth.

Having some trust in an adult.

Not feeling overly deprived.

Having some sense of hope.

Having some attachment to an adult person.

Not feeling too suppressed.

These conditions cannot all be met when a child is admitted. We may have to wait. We may have to do something about the situation, the houseparent, or the child himself before real learning comes from the experiences provided. Cottage parents need to be alert to what children must learn and gain from living together—and also what staff members, especially houseparents, must be like and must do in order to promote this learning.

12. SENSING PERSONAL WORTH

As a child grows, he seeks and finds ways of testing or proving himself in relation to others around him. To become a happy and mature person, he must first be convinced that he is welcome and wanted and that those caring for him will satisfy his wants. As he grows more satisfied and more certain of his place, he can move toward consideration of others and share with others.

Because of various misfortunes, many boys and girls admitted into children's institutions lack conviction of their own worth, value, importance, ability, place. Because they do not have assurance in themselves, they are slow to mature and to enter into good relationships with other people.

Our job is made increasingly difficult because of the meaning that these youngsters attach to their living in the institution, the factors in their lives that cannot be changed, the responsibility placed upon us for many other children as well.

Contributing factors:

The fact of placement itself, if the arrangements were handled poorly or if made under desperate circumstances.

Problems of the family which have caused criticism to be focused upon the child, either back home or in the institution.

Lack of love, care, affection, as demonstrated to the child in his life back home.

Problems of the institution itself, such as change-over in staff or limited opportunities.

Personal handicaps.

Unresolved conflicts regarding family members.

Poor preparation for competition or achievement.

Unpopular traits or characteristics.

These may cause children to:

Reject the idea of living away from home.

Resent authority.

Show extreme jealousy toward others.

Bully, belittle, antagonize.

Fear other children and new experiences and changes.

Continually test the concern of adults for them.

Play on the inadequacies of others—children and adults.

Seek, in every way, to satisfy their own interests first.

Lead others against others.

Give up without trying.

Boast of their own skills and knowledge.

Undermine activities which other children might enjoy.

Withdraw as lone wolves.

Give way to chronic dissatisfaction.

Be unable to tolerate competition or loss.

What can be done?

Engage the family in planning. This most usually is a responsibility of the casework staff and of the administrator. If a child can feel that his family is supporting the placement, carries some responsibility, is recognized, he will capture more of a sense of his own worth.

Engage the child in planning. If he can feel that he had some choice in coming to the institution or can make some decisions or can help plan while there, he will gain some conviction about himself. Pre-placement visits and preparations are so important. Every effort should be taken to avoid having a youngster look upon the placement as a punitive action.

Understand. Not just the child by himself but the people who are important to him; what has happened to him. Only through such an approach can an institution deal with boys and girls who are quite troubled and confused and who do not readily respond. The staff needs opportunities and methods for sharing information and experiences while the child is in placement with the idea of arriving at some mutual understanding of the child as he is, the kind of program and help needed.

Provide consistent framework of living. Through this the young person can find his own place and find something to which to cling until more basic problems yield to some kind of solution. Through this program geared to the needs of most of the children under care, the child can find that he has equal importance with others and that many of his problems are like those of others.

Provide special help. Although we cannot individualize as much as we might like to, it is necessary to give very special attention to the personal problems of children. Staff members carrying special assignments may be in a position to give the more individual consideration needed. These may be possible:

Plan individual contacts with the caseworker.
Locate a special interest or encourage child into an activity.
Assign a youngster to a job which may be satisfying or appealing.
Offer spiritual guidance from a chaplain or pastor.
Give special help with school studies.
Recognize a talent or skill.
Discover a friend for the child outside the institution.
Provide more intensive psychotherapy.
Give a child a responsibility which has an appeal for him.
Arrange special medical treatment or care.
Find opportunity for each child to earn money to pay for personal needs.
Note the need of a young person for an outing and plan for it.
Give him chance for leadership in a group.
Allow for special purchase of an item of clothing.

It takes every staff member. Much of our time is spent, as staff members, in trying to understand and work with youngsters who do not feel right about themselves. Besides doing what we must to deal with situations which arise, we should continually seek ways which will give these youngsters more assurance and security, so that they will not have to feel left out, will not have to take matters in their own hands, will not have to always be testing and proving, will not be pushing themselves out in front to the detriment of others. This assignment of ours is a total staff responsibility.

IV. Training and Discipline

13. BEING A GOOD DISCIPLINARIAN

Every staff member wants to be looked upon as a "good disciplinarian." It has become a mark of success in living and working with children. This is equally true in the teaching profession and in the home. What constitutes a good disciplinarian varies considerably with each individual's judgment, however.

Almost every leader in the field of child care today emphasizes the need for parents and others caring for children to exercise reasonable limits and restraints and controls. Letting the youngster do just what he wants to do with little direction and little control is not regarded as being good or helpful. We still see, of course, the need for some freedom depending upon the age and maturity and personal needs of the child but we recognize the importance of thoughtful and considerate and responsible types of direction and controls. We underscore the requirement of guidance and training being given in the atmosphere of love and affection for the individual.

Are these marks of a good disciplinarian?

A sharp voice and harsh words. This houseparent can subdue an individual or a group, make them listen and stop any undesirable activity.

Children always speak in a formal way, saying, "Yes sir" and "Yes, ma'am," in the presence of this staff member.

Youngsters immediately respond and obey the directives of this houseparent.

This staff member never hears any "back talk," any bad language, any complaints.

Children respond and do what is required by this worker, because she promises them rewards for good behavior.

Boys and girls do not bother this staff member. They steer clear of him except for essentials and do not speak to him in an informal way at any time.

When this housemother is in the cottage, the children hardly ever speak much above a whisper, move quietly about the house, and are always respectful and do their jobs.

At mealtimes children speak only when they talk with this staff member. When an adult is talking, the children keep quiet.

With the help of older children, the other children in the cottage obey.

Youngsters cry when talked to or punished by this staff member.

When away from the cottage, the children follow this houseparent's direction and walk in pairs, even though the houseparent is not around.

A good disciplinarian could not be judged by one incident or a particular method of handling a problem. No one is perfect in always knowing just what to do or how to do it. No one is clearly free from mixed feelings and motivations in dealing with young people.

Our goals are important. Houseparents are trying to help children to gain maximum benefits from their group experience. They want children to find its value now in giving them satisfactions and enjoyment and its value later in having given them the best kind of foundation for adult life. They want to cultivate in young people an ability to discipline themselves, to know what is right and wrong, to want generally to conform to acceptable behavior because of a positive identification with the rest of society, to form good judgment and good sense.

A good disciplinarian, therefore, is one who contributes to this formation of strength and self-discipline. The values will be, for the child, in terms of his present experience and also in terms of preparation for later life.

The houseparent must be alert to the reality of group living, too, recognizing that it is not possible always to work with the group to the benefit of each child. A good disciplinarian will know the total group and be able to make quick judgments as to what action, if any, to take to help children and also to keep a balance in the total cottage situation. Sometimes the houseparent needs to look outside the cottage for assistance from a supervisor or superintendent.

Our focus should be on the benefits to children, rather than upon the way things look to the other staff. It may happen, however, that our judgment of benefits derived by children from our method of handling may be wrong and we may need to clarify our own thinking. We must also remember that a cottage is a part of the institution and there must be an endeavor on our part to bring our group into harmony with the total program. We should have leeway for taking responsibility and using our own judgment, within the broad framework of accepted behavior determined by the staff as a whole.

Guides toward becoming a good disciplinarian:

Participate with the staff in determining the general code for behavior as accepted for the institution as a whole and agree to work within this framework.

Figure out through experience and in evaluation sessions with the supervisor one's own best methods and approaches to disciplinary problems.

Learn to develop an atmosphere of comfortable living, of interesting activity, of congeniality within the cottage. Anticipate and prevent issues and crises before they occur.

Be alert to what is going on elsewhere in the institution and in the community. This will help in making most reasonable decisions.

Be alert to the special needs of individual children, to particular upsets and reasons for them. This will help in taking the most effective approach to helping the child.

Be alert to the group code and group balance, to know what will most likely benefit the whole group, what will gain the best response, what must be done to keep the balance.

Demonstrate fairness by giving youngsters a reasonable chance, the benefit of the doubt, but also take the necessary action when it is best that it be done.

While finding ways of being friendly and interested and having fun, retain one's adult role. This involves consistency toward the important rules and expectations, consistency of attitudes, limiting physical contact and activity with children, demonstrating an identification with other adults and staff.

Choose punishment which will achieve the desired results and that is no more nor less than is desirable.

While being clear in expectations and being ready to set limits and enforce them, find means of continually showing a personal interest in each child.

Take note of serious behavior and do something about it, even if it means talking it over and delaying briefly the decision regarding punishment or other action.

Do not be legalistic or do the same thing about every incident. Give children the general impression that you are confident in your approach and method of handling a problem.

Avoid confiding in individual children within the group about the troubles of another child or clique. Avoid putting responsibility in the hands of children for handling the disciplinary problems of others.

Be direct and fair about action that must be taken but once such action is taken, avoid re-enacting or publicizing the event in general conversation.

When problems are referred by another staff member, a teacher, or a neighbor, accept the information and agree to study these without committing oneself to a particular method of handling.

Seek to handle most behavior problems within the framework of the cottage, but use supervisory and supportive staff primarily for help in clarifying what might be done or in getting support for an action you must take.

Profile of a good disciplinarian:

Shows confidence in ability to live with, enjoy, and control the group of children in the cottage.

Able to set limits without demonstrating severity, harshness, or hostility toward children.

Not thrown or put on the defensive by verbal attacks or insinuations of other adults.

Able to allow children a freedom of movement (within the general regulations of the institution) without too much uneasiness or concern.

Lives in a generally relaxed situation, within which there is no unusual fear of one another and where youngsters, for the most part, can find ways to indicate what may be wrong without causing a group problem.

Able to encourage the majority of youngsters to go along with a reasonable program set up by the institution and involving these children.

Ready to see where special guidance and support is needed; does not feel defeated in going to another staff member for this kind of help.

Able to handle routine problems within the cottage.

Able to allow youngsters to join in other activity of the campus, to be with and associate with other adults.

Has the respect of children as demonstrated by their recognition of requests which are "meant" and by their positive relationship with him.

Can act when necessary and assigns a punishment and means it, without losing relationship.

Finds it easy and possible to look back upon reasons for behavior, see the implications for the child, and yet not feel undue guilt over action which has been taken which was justified at the time and was within reason.

Benefit to children. All children in a group can appear to be disturbed if the houseparent is unable or unwilling or too confused to exercise responsibility toward disciplinary issues. There are many incidents each day of this nature which can be handled firmly and confidently and with understanding. A few occasions reach crisis proportions or become more serious—for an individual, for the cottage group, or for the institution as a whole. The setting and enforcing of limits is an on-going thing and is very much a part of the whole living program for a child and for a group. The adequacy of the houseparent, the richness of the cottage activity, the nature of the group, the way in which physical needs are met—these and many more factors are interrelated with disciplinary conditions, with the necessity for punishment, with the amount of difficult behavior, with the general conduct of the cottage, with the contentment of members of the group.

What one houseparent does as a disciplinarian is related to the other staff as well. The experience of a child with one houseparent will have repercussions with his next houseparent, with his teacher, with the superintendent, with his caseworker. It is important that the houseparent be a good disciplinarian and this requires knowledge about what it takes to be one and the ability to learn and do.

14. OUR DUTY TO STOP THEM AND REDIRECT THEM

As an infant, a child is able to demand and get what he wants— if his parents can figure out what it is he is asking for. He does what he wants to do and fusses and cries if he does not have this freedom. Adults have no function but to serve him and satisfy him. As he gets older, the child is gradually introduced to the expectations and desires of others. His parents begin to decide for him some things which are best. They begin to insist on his fitting in and on his giving recognition to the rights and limits of others. Later on, in his teens especially, the youngster is gradually released from the direction of parents and is expected to carry on more and more for himself but according to the best teaching of his parents. Finally, as a young adult, he finds himself more on his own, ready to make decisions and carry responsibility almost totally for himself.

Throughout his childhood this young person's training has not been left merely to chance. The parent has assumed various responsibilities in directing, in teaching, in guiding, in controlling. Sometimes, these responsibilities have been carried out in rather direct form; at other times, in a more subtle and indirect form. Their impact has been constructively felt when delivered in a *climate of love and affection*. He is able finally to take hold of himself because he wants to, knows values and is dedicated to them, and feels confidence in himself.

Disciplinary procedures. During the process of helping a young person grow and develop, a parent finds it necessary periodically to insist on compliance by a child when the child himself would do otherwise and feels strongly that way. The parent may insist for reasons of necessity, protection of the child, the good of all, the good of the child, the underscoring of what is more important. The child may resist for reasons of convenience, emphasizing his own independence, testing to see the parent's wisdom, pressures of other children, inclination of his own will, attraction to another alternative, or disinterest.

There are times also when a youngster may go against the general direction and guidance received from the parent or may disobey a specific request or demand. The parent may choose various methods of dealing with such situations, depending upon his judgment of the seriousness of the offense or the best ways of getting the child to do better in succeeding instances. Much depends upon the parent's relationship and meaning to the child and his understanding of the child and the circumstances.

In order to get the desired response or action from the child, it may be necessary for the parent to suggest consequences which may include disciplinary measures, or punishment; in order to emphasize to the youngster the error of his ways and the importance that the parent attaches to the mistake, the parent may punish. Effective use of such measures must follow the use of other methods of seeking the youngster's cooperation and participation and obedience. *Punishment usually is necessary only when other attempts fail.*

The aim of punishment is to direct a child's attention to what he has done that is wrong and to arrest his present behavior, to stimulate effort on his part to correct his behavior and to strike out in a more desirable direction, and to let him know that his action has not been approved and that he will have to change or expect further consequences.

When punishment is most effective:

When not too frequent and not for petty offenses.

When it does not involve harsh physical contact, such as hitting or slapping.

When child and adult like one another and have done good things together.

When the adult has made clear efforts to get the child's cooperation.

When the punishment is promptly carried out.

When the situation is handled and then just as promptly dropped.

When the adult keeps the matter out of general conversation.

When the punishment is related to the offense.

When the punishment is not harsher than is necessary.

When the child is not humiliated publicly.

When the adult acts with confidence and not out of frustration, fear or uncertainty.

When there is follow-up to show the adult's forgiveness and readiness to proceed.

When there is fair treatment of the issue.

When judgment is not made too quickly or sharply.

When the punishment is directed toward the real offender and not the bystander.

If the adult is to accomplish more than just arresting the behavior or causing the youngster to behave because of fear of consequences, it is necessary for the child to sense a feeling of personal responsibility for his action and be ready to face this squarely. It is necessary that he not put the responsibility on others or on those who have meted out the punishment. For this reason, the above conditions of punishment are important. Out of this sense of responsibility and desire to change, the youngster can build self-discipline and develop control of his own urges, which is the parent's ultimate aim.

There is bound to be some resentment, at least temporarily, felt by the punished toward the punisher. We cannot avoid this, but can avoid an abiding resentment caused when a child feels mistreated and misunderstood.

Our particular circumstances. Children in the care of a houseparent have not lived with that person since they were young. They have not had the benefit of consistent, continuing care and handling by the same persons. Often they have been exposed to poor experiences. We may have to help change attitudes before we can see a child begin to develop. Some youngsters may have been punished too much and some too little or not at all. Some may have been loved by incapable parents. Some may not have really been loved, but may have been controlled. If children are in serious conflict and are behaving so badly that they cannot be reached by normal effort, it may be necessary to arrest their behavior through a different living arrangement which inherently possesses and suggests more controls.

It is also necessary to consider the presence of the group and the fact that behavior of children is related to the pressures of the group. This is especially a strong consideration when children live together, as they do in a child-caring institution. The individual can sometimes only be reached through action which involves the group, and unfortunately such action may affect children who are not directly responsible for the behavior.

Some methods of punishment that we use:

Deprivation of privilege. (Taking away TV, radio, date night, show, team participation, going to town opportunities.) This is best when not overdone or too frequent. We must consider the implications on others when we take away a privilege that may affect them—such as not allowing a boy to be on a team. We must also consider the individual who needs to have some privilege in order to feel better about himself and want to do what is acceptable. These punishments are best imposed when they relate to the offense —such as depriving a girl of a date night because of overstaying a dating time. Long term campusing or restrictions often deepen a child's feeling of resentment against the institution and produce a sense of hopelessness in him. A "deprivation of privileges" should be a deprivation of a real privilege and not a simple making of life uncomfortable and dull for him.

Curtailing or limiting spending money. When there is misuse of money, this may be imposed. Avoid limiting a youngster so much that he may feel compelled to steal or take to get what he needs. Some money may be for essential needs and ought not to be touched. A child may be expected to pay for deliberate acts or pay for what he has taken by mistake.

Adding extra burdens, jobs. This is best when related to what youngster has done wrong or not done. It can be good if the activity reduces tension through physical exercise or if child learns through the process. Long, tedious, assignments may do more harm than good. Special disciplinary jobs may be developed so as to remove any stigma from other types of employment for which children might normally be assigned or volunteer.

Monotony measures. (Making children write sentences over and over. Sitting in a chair for a long period. Going up and down steps over and over. Memorizing from the Bible, other books.) None of these is too effective, except as there is nothing else and action must be taken. Using the Bible in punishment is not good. If other measures are used, there should be a reasonable limit to them.

Separation from activity, group. (Send to bed. Sit in next room. Firmly lead from the area. Study in another part of the room or building.) This may not always be a definite punishment but may be re-direction of the child out of a disturbing situation and into another group or activity where child might respond better. Avoid sending to bed those children who have an inclination to turn their attentions to their own bodies. A youngster should never be shut in a small room, such as a closet.

Spanking. Mild spanking can be effective with some young children when carried out by persons respected by them. It may be useless for some because of their previous acquaintance with a heavy hand or paddle. It is frequently damaging because of the emotional and sexual implications of physical punishment. It should not be used with teenagers.

Expulsion from group. (Longer-lasting separation from a situation or group. Placement in a special area, a different room for a day or so.) May sometimes be carried out, not as a punishment, but as a change of plan for the child, in an attempt to find a better living arrangement. Supervision required.

Ridiculing, embarrassing, humiliating. These serve only to build greater resentment on the part of the child toward us and other adults.

Scolding. Through words, we attempt to let a youngster know that we are upset by his action, that we feel it is only reasonable to expect a certain kind of behavior from him, that we insist on his changing his ways. This can help, providing our scolding of a child does not become monotonous, and overbearing, and self righteous, and providing we do not use language that hits "below the belt" and attacks tender areas of his life, such as family experience and feelings of inadequacy.

Deprivation of visits to family, withholding of meals. These should hardly ever be used, because they interfere with unquestioned rights and would usually seriously complicate the child's position.

We need to do something. Those who are required to live day-by-day with young people must support their expectations and limits for children with action, at certain times, when these young human beings, as individuals or as members of a group, cannot see the wisdom of these expectations and limits, feel that these are unimportant, or feel more strongly drawn in other directions. It may be quite important that the houseparent do something—and do it promptly and on time. Too often, houseparents are cautioned against specific punishments; they are told—and rightly so—that they can anticipate and prevent many problems and that they can, through a real interest and relationships with children, avoid much in the way of crisis and disturbance; they are often left, however, with few ways by which they can follow through the necessary decisions they must make.

Houseparents need help in seeing what they can do—even though an approach may not be the most ideal or the most desirable one to the needs of the person. The conduct of the group is important to the success of the individual child in it. Therefore, the houseparent's concern logically must be for the group decorum as well as for the affairs of the child.

Attitudes rate high. A specific action by a staff member is not as important as the attitudes felt and expressed continuously by that person toward the child and others. Young people, unless they are seriously disturbed, usually have the ability to recognize the genuine interest and concern of an adult and that person's readiness to help. Let us examine the true sentiment we have toward those under our care. Let us further our understanding of children, so that our efforts can more positively and constructively be given.

15. MAKING THEM READY FOR INDEPENDENCE

As children grow older they want and need to have greater independence of thought and action, so that they will be able to move away from the protective arms of parents or substitute parents and make a go of it on their own. It is difficult even for staff members in a group-care agency to allow young people to take greater responsibility for their own actions. Often, many of these children do not have the beginning ability to make good decisions, and lack trust and confidence in home life and the people there to support them in their independent urges and moves.

Fortunately there are always boys and girls in children's homes and centers, who, like their counterparts in the community, are stable enough to accept as much responsibility as can be theirs and to handle themselves well. A minority of children get confused, tend to over-demand, or follow their own impulses almost completely as soon as they are asked to decide for themselves or as soon as they come upon situations which call for an immediate decision.

How can we fortify children for independent experiences, so that they may more likely act in responsible ways? When are they confronted with a necessity for decision? Perhaps in the following situations:

Choosing suitable companions.
Making dates; conduct on dates.
Procuring goods at stores.
Choice of recreation.
Participation in church life.
Use of money.
Making requests for off-campus visits.

In considering how to influence young people, it is well to look at what determines the choices a person will make:

Concepts of right and wrong. These have been developed according to the teachings and examples of parents, substitute parents, and companions. Most young people have a good idea of what is acceptable behavior and action.

Pressures to be liked and accepted. These may be stronger in some children than in others of the same age. These may be of a special type among teenage youngsters.

Fear of consequences. Fear of what the cottage mother or the supervisor may say or do can have a bearing. It can be a stabilizing force for children although it may not be the best way of encouraging them to think for themselves.

Reaction to leadership. This may apply to leadership exercised by other young people or to adult leadership. The force or attractiveness of a leader may strongly influence decisions, in spite of a child's knowledge of what is right.

General view of society. How does the youngster regard society and the people it includes? If his view is a friendly one, his choices will be different than if he views others as enemies or as being ready to hurt him.

Hope toward future. This will color what a person does. If he feels he has something to live for or is planning toward college or a special job, he will guide his daily actions, to an extent, on the basis of this spirit.

Value placed on an issue. An adult may see a course of action as very important, whereas the youngster may put it in a different category. This sense of values may differ among children too. Some may regard items belonging to the institution as things to be shared or taken, although they might not regard items belonging to a public school in the same way.

Great personal needs. The necessity to a child of having some privilege, some friend, some object, some success may be so overpowering that better judgment is pushed aside.

Urge to test or to experience onself. No matter what others may have told us, there are experiences we strive to have for ourselves to confirm what we believe. This leads some children into making poor choices of behavior, even when they have been warned or guided not to do so.

Attitudes toward present life situation. If a youngster is really happy in the placement or has arrived at some understanding of his predicament, he may be counted on more to behave responsibly, providing he knows what is expected of him. If he hates the institution, feels he is being forced to live there, feels that the Home is keeping him from his people, struggles with his view of family and placement, he may be inclined to retaliate through behavior which is not best.

Obviously, there are steps which the staff of a children's home can take to develop an atmosphere conducive to better decisions and choices on the part of young people. Although these will help most children, there will always be some who must be dealt with separately through very special action in their behalf. These are some of the general steps which might be taken to improve the over-all program:

Staff members being consistent and clear in what they regard as right and wrong, interpreting their opinions, showing this in their own lives—without flaunting their "goodness" or trying to appear as though they make no mistakes.

Keeping clear as to what is most important—religious convictions, philosophy of life—so that just "doing right" is not made the ultimate.

Allowing, as children grow older, for greater freedom of opportunity and decisions for the group as a whole rather than building the program of opportunity around those few who are not ready for it.

Being clear as to what the arrangements and expectations are and then following through on them, to show the importance that is placed on them.

Providing help to children, through individual work, in understanding reasons for placement.

Using group discussion to arrive at understanding, to share ideas and to help young people to feel a part of decisions.

Beginning with young children to offer enough opportunities for adults and children to know and trust one another, and for boys and girls to have wholesome associations with one another.

Sharing with individuals and groups ideas and concerns around important matters which are appropriate to their growing up experiences.

With most children, facing issues in a straightforward way. When a youngster gets in a "jam," acting on it after first getting as much of the whole "story" as is available. Even in the most serious matters where youngsters must be punished or even separated from the Home, trying to conclude with a spirit of forgiveness and understanding and support.

Trying to tie up gifts with persons that the youngsters know and with whom they have some relationship. Developing discussion around the origin and value of facilities, property, equipment, food— without pressing the obligation which the adult thinks the children should sense.

Encouraging members of the staff to be closely associated with the community people in order to gain insight into how the Home's children are accepted and regarded. These associations might provide contacts with persons who can be very effective in guiding young people.

Providing opportunities for youngsters to visit in private families —their own or the families of others. Some children who might feel too pressured in such situations or some families that might make arrangements out of selfish reasons or obligation might not be the best for these experiences.

As much as possible, enabling young people to secure property in most normal and personal ways. Clothing, toys, even food items that are worked for or purchased out of their own money can be most valuable.

Offering ways for children to pay for destroyed property or stolen goods.

Helping young people to know and feel accepted by various staff people and by town people. This will aid them in following accepted patterns of behavior. A boy who is introduced by the superintendent to the manager of a restaurant or a movie house may feel differently toward that place of business the next time he comes.

Dealing tactfully with older children in their relationships to other staff and especially to town people. This will help immeasurably in working with them around their conduct in the community.

Unless a children's institution is specializing in the care of seriously disturbed or delinquent young people, it is right that it should provide many normal opportunities according to age and maturity. These boys and girls need to be able to try out independence on a gradual basis, still having the support and protection that they need of staff members. A few will demonstrate that they need special controls which the institution may have to give. There may be some who create a situation necessitating change of placement. An institution, working thoughtfully and responsibly, ought to be able to follow through with these special arrangements without becoming defensive about them. Its total program should be related to the needs of the majority of those needing its care.

16. ROUTINE CAN MAKE SENSE

All families have a measure of routine, of system, of regulation. Routine, however, is much more recognizable in a group living program. There it may have come into existence out of necessity. Without a system, a routine, a group of children could not live together and the program would soon disintegrate. This routine when it is related to the needs of youngsters served has important values for these young people. Residential programs differ in the extent of routine. Children vary in their ability to make constructive use of it.

What makes up routine?

Procedures for getting up in the morning, for going to bed, for mealtimes, for school attendance, for medical care.

Regulations pertaining to off-campus privilege.

Regular work which is necessary for the operation of the cottage or the institution.

Procedure for obtaining clothing or allowances.

The schedule of regular activity, such as swimming, crafts, tutoring, club meetings.

The plan for Church and Sunday School attendance.

The schedule of "time on duty" for houseparents and substitute workers.

Procurement of supplies.

Rest hours.

Regular outings and recreational events.

The laundry schedule, either out of cottage or within its walls.

The dating plan. Visiting hours.

The method of transacting business in the office. Use of telephones.

What is good about routine?

It clarifies for a child where he fits, where he belongs, and where he carries responsibilities.

It assures him that he will be cared for on a consistent basis.

It encourages him to depend upon others around him and to involve himself with them.

It helps children to see that what is expected of them, in a general way, is also expected of others.

It helps them to see that expectations are group-directed and are not personally-directed.

It gives a new child or a disturbed youngster something tangible to take hold of.

It provides continuity in many areas of life, despite changes in staff or children.

What can be bad about routine? Too long an exposure to a routine may detract from personal development of responsibility and initiative. Routine imposed without thought of those being cared for or of the circumstances can trigger the development of superficial relationships and chronic withdrawal from important issues. Imaginative programming can take a back seat to the traditional, routine approach and plan.

How much routine is sound?

Enough so that:

New children can readily find their way.

The general activities of the day will move along in some order.

Houseparents can feel strength and support in carrying out their work.

All staff and children feel a part of the general organizational framework and not way out of step.

That extent which permits:

Houseparents leeway to make their own decisions, and children to make some of theirs.

The essential work of the institution to be accomplished.

Young people to have time of their own and not feel on the run from one activity to another.

Possibilities of variety and change from time to time.

How do we help children to live with routine? Once we are convinced that our routine is good, constructive, and necessary, we are confronted then with the fact that some boys and girls require help in accepting, in adapting to, and in participating in this regular approach to living. There are times when the routine does not coincide with the desires and impulses of young people and they would choose to fight it rather than join it, or just ride along, without feeling any personal responsibility. What can we do?

Pitch in and work. Join children in an aspect of life that is not appealing perhaps to us as well as to them.

Without fuss, insist that the routine way must be complied with; suggest the consequences and what the child may have to do to make up for his failure. Follow up.

Explain clearly what is expected and, as honestly as one can, the reasons why. Recognize that some routine expectations *are* difficult to understand.

Select responsibilities according to the interest, ability and needs of the boy or girl; vary responsibilities often.

When children are engrossed in an activity, prepare them, if possible, for the end of the activity by reminding them of the time and what will next be required of them, rather than suddenly halting the activity.

In some instances, provide a period of time during which a task may be accomplished, thus allowing for some choice and planning on the part of the youngster.

Determine what parts of the routine need to be rigidly enforced and what parts can be dealt with more flexibly.

Talk to groups concerning their reactions to the pattern of living which is established and the reasons behind it.

Watch for chances to vary the pattern, thus providing a "breather." Learn to anticipate restlessness.

Alert others to a child's concerns and anxieties about family, personal problems or his placement away from home so that he feels more settled and better able to live and accept group life.

Consider, with youngsters, what life might be without rules and regulations.

Encourage youngsters to help one another in participating within the framework which has been set up.

Help each child to find personal outlets, hobbies and interests so that he can better go along with the less appealing, less flexible phases of his existence.

Develop appealing plans for the days to come so that children can look ahead with some pleasure. This will help today.

Where possible, seek the participation of young people in determining what the routine requirements should be. This must be done, however, without houseparents abdicating their decision-making responsibility.

Routine is ours to use. Routine can enable us to live more comfortably with one another. It can serve those who have not settled down, have moved hither and yon, are unsure of their own ability to get along and do for themselves, question the willingness of others to live with them and give daily care with no strings attached, feel that what adults ask of them are personal attacks, or wonder about tomorrow and where they will be then. Every residential program has its own routine ways, some good and some not so good. We might do well to take inventory once a year of our routine and determine whether we have what we want.

V. Children in Groups

17. IT HAPPENS IN GROUPS

In a children's home, young people spend much more time in associations with other young people than is true in most homes or neighborhoods or communities. Some of this association takes place within the framework of well planned, defined groups. Some of it takes place within a rather free, informal, fluid situation. The cottage group is usually the basic unit to which each child belongs. There are variations between the cottage group and other organized groups anywhere, but there are also strong similarities.

In almost any organized group:

The desire of each member of the group to be a part of it varies in intensity.

Some members are more ambitious for leadership; others are content to follow; some feel set apart.

A few, either because of their own problems or because of the group's problems, are rejected.

There is an uneasiness on the part of some members over new members, the role they will play in the group, and the effects that will follow.

Within a larger group, there is a tendency for cliques to develop. These vary in the intensity of relationship, the purpose, and the deliberateness of their formation.

There is a tendency for most members to seek to obey the will of the vocal majority or of those carrying the most prestige.

"Imposed" leadership is accepted after a convincing show of understanding, prestige, skill, loyalty, impartiality, responsibility and interest.

In a cottage group:

Pressure of circumstances has brought the member into the institution and this group. He often thinks he would rather be elsewhere.

Strong influences may exist to draw him and his loyalty away from the group and even to cause him to feel hostile against the cottage group.

Leadership is imposed from outside the group itself and carries many parental responsibilities.

Within the framework of this group, the member is expected to find aspects of home life and to carry responsibility.

Members are assigned to this group and stay with it until someone outside the group moves them.

Group life is a mixture of both group and individual activity.

Participation in other groups and activities are related to the member's part in the cottage group.

The cottage group is determined generally by persons other than members of the group. Its control is really vested in others than members. It offers to each member a place assured by presence of an imposed leader, the houseparent. It provides a base from which the member can move and act but to which he must look for direction and guidance and discipline. It gives experience in living daily with other members under benevolent control and guidance; it allows for an amount of free interaction among members.

The Wish to Belong. This must be cultivated and helped along. Other youngsters must be guided and encouraged to make a place for the newcomer. Unless a boy or girl has this desire to belong, placement in the institution may be of little value. A youngster cannot always be admitted and accepted right away. He wants most of all to be accepted by others of his group, of his age, of his sex. Some children have always had trouble in breaking into and being part of a group. Efforts prior to placement can help, such as in arranging preplacement visits, telling the child accurately and sensitively what the institution is like and what he can expect and how he can approach it, in showing him pictures of the Home and its activities, and getting the parent's participation. Once placed, the child needs frequent reassurance and support in making the change-over and in feeling his way along. Here, both the caseworker and the parent can help. Other, more mature, friendly youngsters can assist. Moves of children to other cottage groups require preparation and guidance, too. Having a meal in another cottage, visiting with the houseparent, spending a day with the children there can help him over this hurdle. Throughout the placement, most children need periodic assistance and guidance in fitting in, and gaining from the experiences with which they are confronted.

Leadership among Children. This is bound to rise up from within. Usually it is good and we like to see it. It may be quite strong on the part of an individual youngster or it may be shared. Leadership may represent conscious effort or it may just happen. It may be for or against adults. It may be of a dominating or of a democratic form. It may take into account what is good for all or what is good for just a few. Leadership may be accomplished through fear. A leader may attract followers through ability or skill or physical qualities which are respected and admired. He may command others by virtue of his wisdom or understanding plus ability to unite their efforts and show the way. He may lead through forms of bribery, by offering advantages in return for obedience. Leadership may be active or may lie dormant until time of crisis or dissatisfaction. A person may lead others through a compelling drive to be on top or to call the signals. He may be skillful in sizing up situations and in reaching decisions and achieving goals. He may have "matured" beyond the others in ways which draw others to him. He may lead out of a desire for power or to hurt others, even those he may lead. There are those, fortunately, who take leadership as a result of maturity, of real ability, of a desire to get benefits for the group which are good and safe.

Those who follow. Most young people are in this category. Some are content and do not aspire to leadership. They may find satisfactions in other ways or they are just happy in getting along. Some may envy the rights that go along with leadership and would like to be on top but lack the drive or the opportunity. They may tie themselves to a leader to get some of the safe advantages. Most children have desires to be a part of the group and follow along after someone they can respect and who respects them. A few in a cottage group may be tempted to tie themselves to the adult leadership, the houseparent, and thus alienate themselves somewhat from the group. The houseparent must be sensitive to the group reaction to children who may appear to be too closely identified with her or who appear to be more loyal to her than to other children. Usually the staff member can cultivate and achieve a trusting relationship with children in a group without causing them to "lose face" with others.

Setting themselves apart. A boy or girl may put himself out on a limb. He may refuse to work at becoming a member of a group. This may be due to his attitude toward being at the Home. He may have made up his mind not to like others. He is obsessed with ideas of being with his family, of going home, of having been rejected by parents. Some may withdraw from group situations consistently. They feel that they cannot succeed. They are afraid of others. They think that others do not like them. They are sad and unhappy. We cannot blame other children for not "taking in" those who will not make the least effort to try to get along. Yet it may be the houseparent's task to help the child to come closer to the group and to help the members of the group to reach out to this individual. Perhaps a bridge has to be built out of an activity, a talent or a friend. Some withdrawn children can move closer to a group by finding support and reassurance in an adult.

The Outcast. A few children just are not wanted and are disowned, rejected, ridiculed, pushed aside, ignored or picked upon by the other members of the group. These individuals want to join in with others but do not know how to go about it. They choose wrong ways and end up offending, criticizing, upsetting, attacking and encouraging ill will. They have not learned what it takes to live with others. They lack sensitivity. They can make life unbearable unless they can achieve some understanding of how to get along with others and unless they can overcome the hostility they possess.

Cliques. One or more of these smaller groups may exist within a cottage. Membership may change with the wind or may stay quite permanent for months. It is natural in a larger group and with older children for some cliques to exist. These occur often through desires to be more intimately known than is possible in a larger group, to feel certain that one is liked and accepted, to be closer to someone with whom one identifies, to talk things over more thoroughly, or to gain support or help with ideas. Often the smaller group is important in helping a person form stronger relationships. The clique becomes a problem to the cottage group and to its own members when it becomes too exclusive, too permanent, too dominating of others. A houseparent must be alert to what is going on and must be thoughtful in the efforts she makes to guide these friendships.

18. GROUP SPIRIT—UP AND DOWN

Once in a while, in working with groups of children, staff members may sense a more-than-normal allegiance of young people to one another, with resistance and antagonism to the total program, to part of it, or toward some children. This can happen also among adults who work or live in groups. It happens among groups of staff members. What occurs among adults, what causes them to generate this undercover, disloyal, disgruntled, vengeful spirit is quite similar to that which occurs among young people. It is well to remember this, as staff members, and to relate this understanding of one's own processes to that of the children living in group-care. Here are some of the conditions which might, if they persist, create group resentments, resistance, negativism, or retaliation:

Strong leadership by an unhappy child. A child who cannot seem to succeed or gain status or find friends through normal procedures or just cannot wait for good things to come may substitute a temporary type of satisfaction gained from pressuring, intimidating, seducing other children into supporting him or in doing things his way. Other youngsters become loyal to this leader, at least publicly, out of fear of him, his exciting appeal, sympathy, or respect for his courage. Possible solutions to this problem lie in appeal to the leader, giving him more acceptable ways of leading, appeal to other children or a re-direction of their interests and change of placement or separation.

Rules which are too strict or too easy. When young people are held to the letter of the law, which to begin with is rigid, they may feel forced to comply on the surface and in the presence of authorities, but may seek other ways of demonstrating their displeasure. They feel, finally, that understanding comes only from companions rather than from adults. When rule enforcement is too lax and indefinite, youngsters feel lost, and unsure children become more unsure. This causes youngsters to bind together or follow unwise leadership in an effort to be safe and protected and cared for.

Punishment that is broad and not interpreted or understood. When this is a consistent approach to young people, there tends to evolve bitterness toward the adult group as a whole and a desire to retaliate in some way against the organization. Too frequent use of group punishment or hasty, extensive action taken after minor skirmishes will push young people away from development of trust and confidence in adults.

Changes or decisions made too hastily or abruptly. Movement of children into an institution or cottage or from one cottage to another may be done in a hasty or abrupt manner, because of an emergency or because of a failure to see the importance of cautious planning.

Complete revision of an activity program or changing the set-up of the institution school or remodeling of the boy-girl dating provisions may come very suddenly and without young people having much chance to give their reactions or ideas. Just as any of these would affect staff members who were not prepared for them, they affect young persons adversely when this becomes the pattern for decisions and actions. Youngsters who have begun to put some faith in the program and the adults may be upset and uprooted. They find they have been duped and will, most likely, put their trust more in themselves or in their friends.

Camaraderie lacking between staff and children. When there is little enjoyment experienced within a cottage between the personalities living there or when the adults as a group do not find much pleasure in the companionship of young people, the ground is set for difficulty. Although adults must still be adults and exercise responsibility when they have to, they need to relax and enjoy the company of the young people around them. They need to be able to recognize and even admit their own limitations, to an extent, not appearing to be perfect, exact, or always right.

Staff members at odds with one another. It is often said that youngsters are quick to sense such discontent. Those who have come from upset and confused family relationships are ready to interpret staff tension as most serious. They need to know that adults may not agree but still can cooperate, that disagreements are not fatal, that there are ways of solving issues peacefully. Children lose faith in adults whom they see bickering or in staff members who express their distaste for other adults either publicly or privately. From this loss, children move to less reliance on what the adults wants or stand for.

Time to be together is too limited. There cannot be relationship without the opportunity for it. Children and adults need time to be together and need to have things to do together. This does not mean that grown-ups should be in the midst of all activity of young people. If everything that is done is routinized and planned, it is possible that many youngsters will not be known as personalities and will not have the chance to develop as they ought. Children have to know that they are on some kind of individual basis with several adults. Otherwise they are more apt to concentrate their relationships among other children exclusively.

Feelings, demands, and drive are assumed to be unreasonable. When staff members become too set in their judgments of the feelings of young people, a barrier is likely to be established and children will often respond with what the adults expect. Many of the ideas expressed by young people may not be realistic or really reasonable to the adult, yet they must be handled in thoughtful ways. Certain reactions are seen as outright rebellion, because of the difficulty in handling or living with them. In fact, they may not be this serious at all.

Supervision has become "snoopervision." There is little question that young people require an amount of supervision in their activities, more so at some times than others and more so for some children or some situations. Adults who do not personally know certain young people are more likely to act in an ineffective, inappropriate way, which gives children the idea they are not trusted or are being spied upon. Sometimes the rules of the institution force staff persons into this position. Children need and really expect adults to know what is going on and to guide them. They will resent and retaliate against efforts to watch their every move or prevent them from choices and decisions of their own. "Snoopervision" pushes young people away from relationships with adults and causes them to place too much reliance upon their ties with other children.

Judgments of people by staff are too prejudiced, dogmatic, or unyielding. Staff members may go beyond good taste in passing judgment on other human beings, insisting on "classifying" people as good or bad. Young people notice this kind of treatment and often react to the person who is this judgmental. They want adults to show their convictions, but to allow some room for the other fellow. Often the judgments passed along adversely apply to the parents and relatives of children. These opinions can force children, no matter how much they might appreciate the opportunities at hand, to seek guidance and leadership elsewhere.

Obligation of children is emphasized too much. It is common among people to resent that which is given out of pity or because someone feels sorry for them and to turn against those who insist on a demonstration of appreciation and a sense of obligation to those who have done good for them. We want children to understand the value of that which they have around them and to know also how it was provided; it should then be up to them to conclude the rest. When the sense of obligation is stressed too much or thoughtlessly, youngsters may turn against those who are trying to be helpful.

The living pattern has become very monotonous. No matter how fine an institution or cottage may be in its program of care, the "sameness" of its program can eventually foster a distaste and an underlying resistance. If the staff members do not make efforts to provide for changes, children will. There is a spirit for some change, for adventure, even for excitement in all children. If they cannot find this within the accepted program of the institution, they will respond quite readily to the call of adventure in other ways. This is especially true when young people live in groups and feel the strength and support of other children. They require hope—something pleasurable and satisfying to look forward to. Some of this can be anticipated and provided for.

No adults are available for confidential talks. Many young people are reluctant to turn to adults who are involved in their cottage life or in on-going affairs of the program. They want to turn to some who know and understand but who are more removed and will keep matters in confidence. Young folks require skilled handling of their personal problems, particularly as they deal with family issues or the reasons for their placement in the institution. Unless they have these adult people to turn to, they will more likely make their problems a matter of general conversation or else "clam up" and keep them to themselves.

There is too little for children to do. In our desire to be good to children, we may leave them too much on their own, hoping that they will choose wholesome activities. Many may have to be "spoon fed" on this responsibility. Left to their own devices, because of shallowness of interest, a resentment toward placement, a need for quick satisfaction, a lost feeling or an overwhelming confusion, they may become embroiled in unacceptable activity or relationships.

These conditions occur in child-caring institutions in different combinations and intensities. The larger the institution, the more alert and conscious the staff members must be to ideas generated by young people and to interpretations given to children of new policies, actions or changes. Unless staff members can approach their work with optimism and positiveness, their efforts will be wasted. Most children can be reached. Most children can be helped. Most children will cooperate and take interest. Most children can come to trust.

19. SUCCEEDING WITH CHILDREN IN GROUPS

There is a difference between working with a child by himself and working with him as a member of a group. "If I could just live with him alone, it would be easy. I would not be concerned. He would act differently. I know that I could reach him." Perhaps we could, perhaps not. When a young person becomes a part of a group of children living with or reacting to us, we may discover that our influence as an adult is reduced, neutralized, fought or covered up. Almost mysteriously, we find that the weight of a child's associations with other youngsters seems to be so much more than that of his associations with us. Is this really so? Is there anything that we can do or should do?

Boys and girls in group-care are exposed to many more hours of group associations than children in private family homes. Acceptance by other children takes on special significance. The position of the adult has a much different meaning. Although there are adults who have importance to them, institutional children spend more time than do most other children in activities with other children, in their cottages, on the playground, in school, in the dining hall, in church, at club meetings, at work, on outings, on the "junior staff," on shopping trips. Children are influenced in various ways, in individual ways, by their relationships within these group activities, as well as by their relationships to and with the total institution body.

In addition, these young people find themselves in a world of adult influence, of rules and regulations determined oftentimes by others. These do not always agree with the desires, decrees, or activities, or standards of young people functioning or planning together. Each child, on the basis of his own lights, determines how to respond.

Membership in institution groups is not the same as membership in groups out in the community. The factor of 24-hour residence in the children's home affects the nature of the group opportunities afforded children who live there.

These group experiences, though different and more numerous for young people placed away from home and living on a residence basis in a children's institution, often have most important values for these children and their uniqueness makes it possible for many of these boys and girls to make use of them for great personal advantage. We want, therefore, to capitalize upon the strength of groups and use this for the benefit of our boys and girls. The board and the staff have to take the initiative for studying and determining the pattern of group life within the institution so that maximum benefits can be realized.

New workers in children's homes are most perplexed, it seems, by the responses they receive from groups of children—youngsters who have lived together or worked together or played together, who have had other new staff members before, who know their way around. Their responses to the new staff member may be partially determined by the following:

Composition of the group itself.

Recent experiences with other adults including the departing staff.

Assurance of individual children in the responsibility of the administration, that they will be cared for, that someone "up there" in the front office understands.

Quality of the program in which children participate.
Approach of the new staff member.

Just to get to "first base" is important to new workers. They want to feel that they are making some progress, that they are able to fit in and carry their responsibility. The adult's part in the life of children is very important. The adult, however, does not begin to have real meaning for children just by assuming a job or a responsibility.

Striking out. We may miss repeatedly in our work with children in groups if we:

Just oversee and "snoopervise."

Show lack of faith in individuals or in the group, or if we expect the worst.

Emphasize the badness of what is said and done.

Employ harsh, unreasonable punishment.

Lose our own composure too often.

Act with too much reserve.

Preach too much.

Pretend to be more assured than we are.

See "the end of the world" in all wrongdoing.

Expect to be trusted and loved right away.

Give in out of fear or lack of confidence.

Label other groups as bad.

Forbid normal associations among children.

Play up to a few individuals in the group.

Make too rigid, quick, prejudiced judgments.

Consistently use loud, bitter retorts.

Avoid any clear limits.

Too frequently announce new demands and expectations, without preparation.

Ignore children's need for aggressive activity and do not provide places for it.

Break up all cliques and work at separating children from one another, when this is too obviously done.

Dominate and command.

Over-indulge children.

These approaches can force children to choose between the adult and the child leader, to draw the battle line, to resent the presence of the adult and what she stands for, to question the understanding of adults for them and for the rest of the group, to bind themselves more closely to one another out of loyalty and sympathy, to prevent the adult from gaining entry to the real ideas and feelings existing among young people, to deny any feeling for the adult or any need for satisfactions that might come from associations with the adult, and to seek ways of undermining or embarrassing the adult and thus gain the approval of one another.

Getting to first base. The following suggest ways of approaching groups of children and of beginning to obtain results:

Show an understanding of the desires, drives, and pressures which draw children together.

Take a firm stand on major issues, avoiding personal reflections where possible.

Follow through in a reasonable way on demands and requests of individuals and groups.

Encourage and support constructive group activity and even help to initiate it.

Recognize leadership within the group without labeling it as a monster and something to be afraid of.

Act sincerely, honestly and reasonably in making changes or setting limits.

Become as familiar as possible with each child under care and make some opportunities to associate with each one individually.

Allow for group discussion of some issues and even for group decisions or recommendations when such responsibility can realistically be placed in the hands of young people.

Develop one's own prestige through interests, activities, hobbies and friends.

Show a wide tolerance of ideas and activities, without giving up one's own standards or ideas.

Though protecting and taking pride in one's own cottage group, show an understanding for and tolerance of other groups on campus.

Take the initiative in changing routine, breaking the monotony and thus avoiding natural group reaction.

Maintain an optimism about children no matter what they have done and do not reflect long upon children who have gotten into serious difficulty. Take action without fanfare.

Avoid taking one's own self so seriously that one's sense of humor and ability to laugh and take kidding is lost.

Do not use group punishment any more than is necessary and avoid humiliating or denouncing one person in front of the group.

Avoid using one's own cottage group for venting one's own gripes and complaints.

Bring in new, fresh ideas from time to time and point to bright spots ahead.

Be a part of the activity life of the cottage without developing a "buddy" relationship with any of the youngsters.

Show a respect and liking for other children or groups which have associations with this cottage.

Seek out individual help for some youngsters who are especially unsettled and unsuccessful in the group.

In matters of discipline, be firm and prompt and reasonable.

Show loyalty to one's own cottage group, not condemning its members in ordinary conversation with other staff members.

These approaches will allow children to go along with the adult and to like her without losing place with other children, permit them time for choosing how they will relate to one another and to grownups, show them that the adult has understanding and has the interest of children at heart, draw a respect from the group which will enable the majority of children to look to the adult for leadership, indicate the confidence and ability of the adult to carry responsibility and make some binding decisions, assure children that they can subscribe to the grownups' wishes without being embarrassed or losing face or being disloyal, offer them support, on an acceptable basis, from the adult in working out the best relationships with others and in choosing the best avenues for behavior and show the adult's willingness and ability to help in finding solutions and compromises.

20. INDIVIDUALIZING IN A GROUP

Houseparents in children's institutions are, by and large, sensitive to the needs of individual boys and girls. They are often frustrated by their inability to do for a child what he seems most to need or want. With experience, these staff members come to realize that this inability may be the result of the child's own problems, of the houseparent's difficulties, of the family's influence, or of the institution's organizational limitations. We say, today, that institutions for children have a special function, that they offer systems of group living in which youngsters can be helped with their problems or in connection with which families can work out some of theirs.

Cottage living and other group experiences are complex and involve combination of relationships—not just relationships between children themselves. In most institutions, youngsters come to stay for a period of at least a couple of years, perhaps more. Some of these young people come because they themselves could only use a living experience including many other children and free of strong parental demands. Some come because the other people in their family constellation insist on group-care or because no other resource is available; these children could use more personalized care.

Very few youngsters need or could respond to being in a group all the time. Most boys and girls need a balanced diet of group and more individualized experience. In any event, they all require that the program be geared toward meeting personal needs, whether through groups or individual activity. Group living is worthwhile only insofar as it is constructive to most of those who are a part of it. There must, therefore, be an individualization of care. How can this take place? The following are examples of how a house-parent can meet this requirement:

Spending time with the newcomer, introducing him to other children, showing him his bed and closet, handling thoughtfully his concerns regarding personal belongings that he has brought along.

Keeping in contact with teachers and others regarding the actual experience of children; showing an interest in other activities of the child.

Visiting school to see where the youngsters sit and what their work looks like. This can be made practical through special days set aside for visiting in the school.

When worried or perplexed by physical limitations or symptoms of a child, contacting the nurse or seeking more professional help and guidance.

Recognizing when a youngster needs time by himself and trying thoughtfully to arrange for it.

Doing something special for a child's birthday, sending a card when he is sick in the hospital, recognizing some success of his.

Doing all that is possible to preserve the treasured personal belongings of children. Offering to protect the most important things.

Suiting punishment, where possible, to the needs of the child or to what will be most understandable.

Giving girls guidance on dress or hair style. Offering to help them with it.

Finding or creating a responsibility for a child who feels lost and incapable.

Guiding a boy who provokes cottage-mates through his boasts or taunts.

Guiding cottage-mates to handle constructively the child who finds it hard to fit in.

Helping individuals to be more acceptable to others, through manner of dress or keeping clean.

Removing a youngster from a crisis situation.

Showing friendliness and understanding toward a child's family.

Helping a child to find the best place to study and helping him with his homework.

Offering a boy or girl time for private conversation that will be fairly free of interruptions.

Remembering children in special ways or finding gifts that coincide with particular interests.

Answering questions pertaining to physical growth or sex.

Protecting a child from the unreasonable demands of the group, another staff member, or his family.

When a youngster returns from a visit, allowing for irritability or failure to do work well right away.

Listening and showing interest in details of activities on the playground, in gym or at the craft shop.

Ferreting out child's hobby or talent and encouraging and furthering it.

Fixing food according to likes and dislikes. Allowing for some choice at mealtimes.

Supporting a youngster at a time of unhappiness or upset—in hearing of the death of a parent, in learning family members cannot have him for summer vacation.

Helping younger child to read and understand mail.

Giving guidance in use of spending money.

Offering opportunity for participation and expression in devotional periods and prayers.

Finding the best way of dealing with a child's special problem of bed wetting, nail bitting, or daytime soiling.

Understanding when a child may be particularly sensitive and embarrassed; showing tact in dealing with these situations and helping child to overcome these feelings.

Recognizing the best way of meeting complaints—by listening only, acting on them, or helping person to sort out his real reasons for complaint.

All of the acts of individualizing should be based, by the houseparent, on as thorough an understanding as possible of the child as a member of his own family, as a "placed" child, and as a member of the cottage or institution group. This understanding can be enhanced through a sharing relationship with the caseworkers and through the process of joint staff planning and consideration.

VI. Activities and Other Problems

21. WORK AND PLAY

Boys and girls need opportunities for both kinds of activity, for both work and play. The character of either may vary depending upon the needs, age, and maturity of the child. Work and play experiences are closely related and may be quite similar in what they give; yet the child may profit from one type of experience in a way that he could not from the other.

What is play? Play is a child's effort directed by himself and out of his own choice, most usually, into activities which bring him a considerable amount of pleasure and satisfaction and which are pursued primarily for the enjoyment gained in the process of doing the activity. There are results and goals, but the emphasis is on the fun in participating and doing. Some activities may be very free and open in terms of structure; some may be much more organized and defined in procedure. Play activities when they are more developed and coordinated often fit into a "recreation program" which may offer a number of opportunities but still emphasize the voluntary nature of participation and the fun and enjoyment that may be had.

What is work? Work is a child's effort directed, sometimes by himself and sometimes by others, into activities which have definite goals and results, which contribute most usually to the general good or livelihood or to the continuance or improvement of surroundings and which call for certain methods and procedures in the actual performance of the activity. Work usually involves a routine, a responsibility, a necessary task. There is more emphasis on the result, goal, or achievement, although there is profit to be gained by the child through actual doing of the job. Often work is assigned and there is an element of supervision by others.

Work and play may possess similar values:

Release excess energy, tension.
Contribute to physical and emotional and intellectual growth.
Teach good citizenship and sportsmanship.
Create mutual interest, the desire to share and pull together.
Teach differences of others and how to live with these differences.
Develop skills.
Develop self-control.
Develop leadership qualities.
Bring a sense of achievement and satisfaction.
Provide a chance for self-expression.
Provide ways of working out conflicts, frustrations or hostilities.
Provide outlets for aggressiveness.
Offer ways of gaining status, approval, recognition.

What may be the unique contribution of work?

Teaches responsibility for one's own livelihood and that of others.
Establishes a pattern for effort and for doing necessary and important things.
Offers lessons in what it takes to produce goods and services.

Shows what a youngster can do for himself to work out his own future needs.

Helps children to understand that all of living is not just a matter of personal whim and choice.

Work is best when the child can see it as a fair expectation or assignment and when it is within his ability and readiness to do it, when the length of time and the effort required take into account the maturity of the young person, when the youngster senses a responsibility and is helped to see it, when there is some choice in the method of performing the task, when there is participation by adults, when the child has been first taught some beginning skill upon which other skills may be acquired, when the goal is realistic and within sight, and when respect, patience, and approval by adults are mixed in.

What may be the unique contribution of play?

Stimulates imagination and creativity.

Develops healthy, safe, and enjoyable ways of using leisure time.

Draws out a variety of skills and talents.

Allows a child to use his own initiative in thinking through ideas and in reconstructing events and relationships so as to better deal with them.

Offers greater opportunity for free expression of feelings.

Play is best when a youngster sees many opportunities for choice and for use of his own skills and imagination, when leadership is able to indicate possibilities within activities and stimulates genuine interest, when necessary materials and equipment are available and maintained, when a child is helped to anticipate and see the possibilities of the activity, and when personal need is answered or met.

Activities in a child-caring institution. Who are the boys and girls who live with us and what do they need in the way of activity? As we think over our cottage or institutional program, we must remember:

These are children with normal growth and developmental needs. They want to be like other children. They require opportunities for physical development—use of big and small muscles. They need chances to learn about the world and be related to it, and chances to mingle and associate with the opposite sex, as well as with their own. There is a need for individual and group pursuits, and desire for adventure, for that which is different and new. They require gradual introduction to responsibilities, privileges and rights. They can profit from chances to work and play with adults and thus get to know them. They want to go places and see, to learn about themselves, to develop their own coordination. They need to develop talents, abilities, skills, to make choices as they grow and to feel that their own ideas have merit, to be exposed to new views, ideas and possibilities. They have varied interest spans.

These are children who live in groups. They seek ways of gaining acceptance, of belonging. They are easily distracted by others, more ready to respond to adventure's call. They react to the monotony of living, need help in getting along together, in playing and working together, respond best when expectations are made of all in the group. There is a tendency of some to hold back normal expression because of group pressures and a need for activity which crosses clique lines, which helps the isolate or outcast or "fringe child" find ways of succeeding, and leaders to find acceptable ways of leading, of taking responsibility. They respond as a group to unfairness or lack of preparation. It is harder for them to have opportunities for private activity, or to protect their own interests. They tend to ridicule the unsuccessful child. They need to participate in planning, respond negatively to the imposition of activities but positively to the leader who knows and is skillful. They require free time and planned time, and react against spending too much time with groupmates.

These are children with special personal and family problems. They may have conflicts about separation from their families and about placement away from home. They may be harder to reach in terms of interests or talents, may be preoccupied or worried, so that daily effort is retarded. They may have difficulty with other children, with authority, with adults, with assuming responsibility, with acting out or with self-control, may be suffering from past disappointments and failures insofar as activities are concerned, may be reluctant to express themselves, may react with unusual amounts of jealousy, impatience or dread of failure, may require strong encouragement in order to play or work. The interest span for many children may be much shorter than others of their age group. They may need special consideration and activity following visits or when visits do not occur.

Guides for achieving a balanced work and play activities program:

Develop these around the basic requirements of the educational, vocational training, and religious programs.

Make cautious use of the school's extra-curricular program, making it possible for young people to participate, as others, in activities of interest to them, as long as this does not detract from the help which young people should gain from the institution's own program.

Place stress on the contribution which each child should make to his own living quarters, his own cottage or house, his cottagemates and houseparent.

For children up to the age of 12 (approximately), emphasis, normally, in connection with after-school hours should be on the child's play activities.

Children above the age of 12 (approximately) need and can use some work responsibility for one or two hours after school.

An institution should not be dependent upon child labor, although the work of young people should be conceived of and designed as important and valuable work and assigned appropriately.

Stimulate variety through changes in assignments, types of activities, and schedules.

In play, numerous opportunities for activity should be made available; these should be offered on as voluntary a basis as possible.

Devise activities which may throw a youngster in with children other than those in his own group or age group, or which might bring him into contact with community children. Seek activities which bring children together in normal activity, on a normal basis, with children living out in the town.

Provide activities which bring boys and girls together for wholesome experiences.

Plan some jobs for pay and some jobs off campus for more responsible youngsters, so long as these do not interfere with important contributions to campus life.

Avoid using work as punishment too often or indiscriminately.

Join in the activity of young people, wherever possible.

Be ready with seasonal experiences and events. Build up interest. Draw out ideas of young people in advance and seek their help in planning ahead.

Develop a master plan for year-round activities and events. Build in certain traditions.

Allow for a clean-up day, such as Saturday morning. Plan especially leisure time activities for Saturday and Sunday afternoons and evenings.

Improve one's own competence in activities in which one is involved. Children like a carpenter to be a good one, a housemother to be a good housekeeper, and a cook to be a good cook.

Certain monotonous, essential work may require a system or a routine for getting it done. It may not be possible to get enthusiasm or real interest.

Stimulate activities, projects, and hobbies on a cottage level especially. Each cottage or home should have an activity budget and may need help in planning for outings and other special activities.

Avoid imposing on the willing or available youngster.

Prescribe a reasonable but not an endless amount of time for an activity. Close it off when interest has reached a peak.

Expect effort from children but make allowances for those who cannot do or for moods or unusual upsets. Other children understand.

Try to prepare children ahead of time for extra duties.

Avoid having children wait on adults, or do personal things for them, unless there is clearly an exchange of help between adult and child and the child views his effort as something he likes to do but does not feel bound to do.

Seek ideas which can make routine work more interesting.

Offer honest praise.

Older children may help younger ones when mutual interests are served.

It pays to plan ahead. Just as a teacher prepares herself for the lessons to come, houseparents need to prepare for the days to come with ideas, skills, equipment, and know-how for doing things with children. The houseparent's concern is with children who reside with her and this makes for some difference. She needs, however, to hold plans in readiness, so as to take advantage of an opportunity.

22. DOING WHAT OTHER CHILDREN DO

It is natural that young people living in children's institutions should have many of the same needs and demands as children living out in the community. There is greater communication now between institutional personnel and people in the community than in years gone by. There is greater turnover in population, both of children and of adult workers. Television, newspapers, movies, school activities and classes, church activities, all have made children in institutions aware of the experiences, opportunities, and activities available in the community at large. Actually, children's homes are encouraging as much mixing in the community by their children as can be practically managed and controlled and which will be constructive.

Community participation has not come easily. Many youngsters are living in group-care because they have not been able to absorb or satisfactorily confront the experiences of the normal community; they have needed protection, or special guidance, or freedom from stimulation, or more firm direction and controls.

To provide experiences or activities for one or two children has had an impact on a large number of other children as well, in the same cottage, of the same age group, in the same institution, of the same family. When a "yes" has been given, it has had to be based upon a policy which could be applied to others as well.

The institution staff does not work from the same basis which a family does in giving permissions or in considering new experiences for children.   For the houseparent or the superintendent, this is someone else's child.   This youngster probably has not grown up with the same adults, and the trusting relationship that might exist with a good parent is not here.   The youngster does not feel the same allegiance to the institution as he does to his own family. Sometimes a youngster because of his problems is looking for too quick a solution to his placement worries, to his future, and may jump into an unwholesome relationship out in the community or be steered too easily by others who do not have his best interest in mind.

Too much of the youngster's time may be involved in community participation so that the real contribution of the institution is minimized, because he has no real relationships there.   The institution may be trapped into reducing its own program to almost zero.

Because the houseparents and the superintendent usually are themselves removed from the normal swim of the community, they are not always in a position to know and understand what is best, what a situation is like, what the good parent in the community is doing or agreeing to.

Around what do questions arise?

Dating.   Having the same opportunities as children out in town, the same date nights, the same hours, and the same means of choosing dates.   The use of cars.   Attending the same kind of functions— dances, for example.   Going to the next town.

Off campus jobs.   Having the same after school, weekend, and vacation opportunities.   Free choice of where to work and what to do with earnings.   Freedom from campus responsibilities in order to do so.

Recreation.   Participation in school activities of a recreational nature, on teams—placing these events first above the requirements of the institution.   Going to public swimming pools when desired. Traveling in cars driven by other young people.   Having money to pay one's way.

Visiting.   Chances to visit in homes of friends, to stay overnight, or to go for a weekend.   Being free from supervision from one's own people at these times.

Clothing.   Dressing like the others in school.   Being able to buy at stores and to choose one's own style and colors.   Wanting the same quantity and value.

Money.   Spending money to use for special purchase or for admission to functions.   Seeking others with considerable funds.

Home life.   Asking for arrangements in cottage which approximate arrangements in a private family.   Privacy.   Freedom from routine arrangements, and from jobs set after school.

Smoking.   Freedom to smoke in and around the cottage.

What is behind these demands and requests?

These usually come from the older youngster or from the one who is more sophisticated or who has lived a large part of his life in the community.

They express his desire to be like others of his age group.

They may, in part, indicate his recognition of difference, his hostility toward the idea of placement, his restlessness and dissatisfaction.

They may be tests of our assurance, as staff members, as to whether or not we are really interested in young people and want to do right by them.

They may be tests of our limits, of our conviction about their reasonableness, of our ability to hold to them.

They may be related to what children in exceptional situations are able to do, and do not always reflect the life and experience of children from the more average, normal home.

How do we know what to allow?

First, we want to keep ahead of us the goal of preparing all children for eventual return to a more normal living situation in a family, out in the community. We want to provide each youngster with as close-to-normal experience in daily living as possible, as long as this is in concert with the particular helping job we have to do for the majority of children under our care.

We should get clearly in mind the group of children who are to be served by our program and the general needs of this group. This will help to determine where the program's primary emphasis should be, how much community-related it can be and still accomplish its major goals. We can figure out what it is that these children and their families especially need from us and how this is going to be done.

We can check the balance of the program to see that children and staff have a variety of experiences and relationships to meet their needs. Every institution does not arrive at the same answers to each question.

We can help youngsters to get the fullest benefit from any community program to which the institution is committed. (If children go out to school, they should have the opportunity of taking part—as much as possible—as other children do.)

We can become acquainted with stable, good families in the community and get ideas from them as to what is permitted in their families and what they consider to be good. This information, of course, must be related to the institutional program and the essential requirements of its program in order to figure out how much like the community families the cottage group can be.

We can be honest and realistic about what the institution can do and can afford. It may help just to show a desire to do more or differently.

We can keep in mind that the institution cannot duplicate the family. We can recognize the importance and value of general rules and organization which provide a measure of security for young people. Although always open for evaluation and staff consideration, we can keep consistently to a general framework of activity and regulation which is clear to young people.

We can draw together representatives of young people for discussion around certain issues, to draw out their ideas without necessarily placing responsibility for decisions in their laps.

Meeting these demands. Many times they are legitimate requests. They may have to be explored by some staff member. Young people need to discuss these ideas, to try to understand. They do not always agree with us at the time. Yet there are many occasions when staff members, after considerable consideration of a question, must hold firm. There are privileges that would be good for one, but not for many. The houseparent must think of the situation likely to develop. The handling of these demands and requests and questions becomes one of the most important and crucial aspects of the job of the staff member who is working with older children.

23.   BOYS AND GIRLS TOGETHER

Our interest is in providing the kind of climate in which young people can prosper and get the foundation necessary for being happy and responsible adults, in which they can correct faulty training which they have had and overcome some of the conflicts that have developed for them. Everyone should grow into the type of person who feels comfortable in being with the opposite sex, who is able to associate with the other, who can move into intimate relationships when appropriate and acceptable to do so, who can be friendly and yet reserve intimacy for a marriage relationship, who feels no undue curiosity or drive to take advantage or to misuse another physically, who does not stand in fear or hostility of the opposite sex.

It is normal for children to:

Get some of their views of the opposite sex from their own relationships with the parent of the opposite sex and also from observing the relationship existing between father and mother.

Express curiosity at a very early age concerning physical differences.

Accelerate interest in the opposite sex as they approach their teens, and, if a girl, to show interest sooner than the boy.

Throw themselves less judiciously into the path of the opposite sex during early teen age years but with more confidence and assurance and yet with more caution later on.

Give boy-girl relationships a position of prominence in thoughts and ideas during the adolescent period of development.

Seek acceptance, if a girl, through appearance primarily; if a boy, through knowledge of the world, athletic ability, job skill, physical strength, and use of language.

Parents are advised, with their own children, to:

Prepare children well when they are younger so as to build up a basis for trust.

When children are older, seek to guide them but not tell them too much what they ought to do or believe.

Make home a place where boys and girls can be together, where children feel they can bring their friends.

Seek to know their children's companions.

Keep lines of communication open.

Set limits when necessary but try to keep to a minimum arbitrary rules. Allow opportunities for choice.

With young children, offer them chances in the home to be physically close to one another to allay some of the curiosity that will otherwise naturally develop.

Pecularities of the institution's problems. Children who are not related and who have not grown up together live in close proximity to one another. Some youngsters who have tremendous needs for affection may seek to meet these through close physical relationships with others, of their own sex or the opposite sex. It is hard to produce a normal situation because of group requirements. Children move from one cottage to another, and may not have built up the feeling of trust in the houseparent that may be needed. Some older children who feel unsuccessful (in failing to complete school or to perform a job) may be too anxious to find solutions through early marriage. With so many, it is hard for staff members to be close to a youngster's thoughts and to offer opportunities for personal talks. Boys from the outside who seek dates may be bothered by the "red tape" required for dating girls. Not all staff members are understanding or able to talk with young people about boy-girl companionships. There may be more of a drive, because of the group living situation, for children to grow up faster so as to be accepted by older children. Many young people have, prior to coming to the institution, observed in their own families or in neighborhoods intimacies of men and women, boys and girls; they carry the details of these experiences into the institution community. They may have been more personally involved.

The part our own attitudes and knowledge play.   The attitudes of staff members very easily come to the surface in the way that they handle boy-girl relationships.   Some are very fearful of what might happen and although they would not put it into words, they are afraid of the worst.   They imagine that if boys and girls are together they might get off by themselves and indulge in intimate sexual relations or exploration or heavy petting.   Some have confidence in the general good sense of young people who have been allowed to have normal experiences of being together and these adults do not worry too much, except to be responsible in permissions and supervision. A few staff members may be too much identified with young people so that they cannot guide them or are not alert enough or just do not care.   Most adults feel some discomfort in talking with older teenagers about their affairs.   They feel uncomfortable in answering questions regarding the physical makeup of the body or the sexual experiences of people.   Many persons are uncertain as to how to deal with homosexual problems, with natural curiosity acts of children, with exhibitionism in children.   Much of this dates to one's own upbringing and one's own experiences in having such matters hushed up.   Most adults will agree, in principle, with the idea of boys and girls being together in constructive and wholesome experiences, but they differ in the type of activities regarded as constructive, in the amount of supervision which must be given, in their judgments of what a boy and girl mean to one another.

When are boys and girls most likely to get into poor relationships together?

When they have no talents, interests, or skills by which they can feel successful, respected.

When as young children they have had too little physical affection shown by adults around them.

When they have not had normal experiences, in growing up, of being in the frequent company of children of the opposite sex.

When there are too many restrictions, too much obvious prevention of contacts between boys and girls.

When exposed to poor standards of experiences of adults or other children.

When one person is attractive to another and yet regards that person, as well as others, as unimportant and someone to take advantage of.

When there is a lack of trust and understanding between adult and child.

When other children do not realize the importance of a youngster to his or her family or to those with whom she is living.

When a boy or girl is unpopular.

When those caring for a youngster have been unreceptive to his friends.

When there is too much poor control lodged in the hands of the members of the group.

When youngsters are exposed to too much physical stimulation or too much temptation in the way of unsupervised, dimly lit areas.

When there is not enough program, activities, or opportunities.

When the approach of adults is too negative or too punishing.

Some guides for encouraging and insuring good boy-girl relationships:

Reasonable dating rules.

Some mixing of younger boys and girls in cottages.

Playground space where boys and girls can play freely together.

Removal of buildings, not used, which offer too many dark corners.

A lounge or soda shop or youth center, open frequently under supervision, where boys and girls can engage in activities.

Mixed swimming.

Discouragement of public expression of familiarities among older children.

Plenty of opportunity for physical exertion.

Mixed parties in cottages or elsewhere.

Chances to associate with other acceptable young people in the community.

Help children to dress as others do, in clean and attractive clothing.

Identification through group conference, of those young people who need the closest attention and supervision.

An effective person to guide the youngsters in their relationships.

A climate in which youngsters can raise questions, as they have them, concerning sex and related issues.

Opportunities for dancing which is wholesome and can be approved by constituency.

Mixing in central dining room.

Recognition of children's need to be popular and to be accepted by others of their age group, and those of the opposite sex. Help to the child in meeting proper standards.

Help in developing skills and talents which will be good approaches to this need of theirs.

Participation of the children in the normal activities of the community, so that they are inclined to pick friends through these more wholesome experiences.

Firmness when we have to say "no" without doing so in frustration and with apparent uncertainty. Follow up of troubling situations.

Permission for older children to sit together, when feasible, in church and on the school bus.

Opportunities for children to observe family life, on campus and off campus.

What can be done toward guiding these children into satisfying and acceptable relationships with the opposite sex will have a lot of effect upon their future happiness and success.

24.   CHILDREN WHO DO NOT LEARN THEIR LESSONS

Houseparents, as well as teachers and parents, are perplexed these days by what appears to be an ever-increasing number of boys and girls who do not learn or move along normally in their school studies. The larger classrooms in our public schools create a dilemma for the teacher who wants to give individual special help but who finds herself unable to do so. Parents feel tortured when their child does not incorporate knowledge even though he puts his mind, apparently, to his studies. Houseparents can be lost, with a large number of children in their care, in providing the right kind of help to them. What is the answer? The houseparent can blame the teacher for not having patience, for not showing skill or not being interested. The teacher can blame the houseparent for the same reasons. In the meantime, many children move along in age but not in scholastic achievement. The day of reckoning approaches all too fast when the school can no longer put up with the child and the child finds he can no longer put up with the school.

There are different shades:

Some will not study under any conditions. They may sit and look at school books, if we insist.

There are those who try and try, but just do not grasp the material.

Some children study to please or satisfy the houseparent, but do not bother to produce in school or even turn in completed homework.

Some will study but are readily distracted by other children.

A few want to apply themselves but are preoccupied with other ideas.

Some see wisdom in accomplishing the lesson but look for devious, dishonest ways of doing this.

Some children can learn but block in a certain subject.

What are the reasons for poor school performance?

A child may be below average in intelligence or on the border line.

Fundamentals have not been learned during the normal process and may now prevent achievement based upon having information or skills.

The youngster may be more concerned about other matters, such as family, athletics, girl friends or boy friends, or jobs.

The child may be very confused about all that has happened to him and is unable to settle down to any sustained effort.

Because of a long line of failures and disappointments, he may not see much use in frustrating himself with additional effort which does not have immediate and valuable rewards.

His present living arrangement may be so distasteful or unhappy for him that he cannot study.

Some are unable to grasp a subject because of deeper emotional implications, not readily understandable.

A few may be hostile toward any type of formalized situation, or toward anyone in a position of authority, such as a teacher in a classroom.

Some, because of higher intelligence, are not challenged and do not find satisfaction in the work at hand.   Therefore, they lose interest.

Poor study habits may plague some who have never been encouraged in school work or have never had much chance for effective study.

What it means to be a poor learner:

He feels intense pressure to defend himself, to blame others, to pretend adequacy, to indicate that his failure is deliberate.

Besides losing in academic success, he may lose status and friends.

He finds himself growing in size with others of his age group but lacking in grades and achievement.

As he progresses in the school system, he is caught when he realizes how one subject is interrelated with others.

If he cannot stay in school, he may be in danger of losing his home or his substitute home.

He notices the misgivings and reservations that adults develop toward him in other areas of life because of his poor school work.

Because of his normal drives to do other things as well, he is unwilling to relinquish the extra time or energy needed to get special help.   Also, such special help may not be available.

He loses out because so many rewards are based upon school performance.

The youngster is caught in a vicious circle.   He can not achieve in school because he is not convinced he is really liked; he finds that he is not liked because he does not achieve in school.

How we find out what is really wrong:

Through:

Testing for intelligence and school achievement.

Expert study of child's personality and functioning.

Consultation with teacher, special teacher, guidance counselor, or principal.

Observation of and conference with child by various staff.

Conference with family members who have an influence.

We may find out:

His potential to succeed in school work.

His actual performance in various areas of school work.

His ability to get along in his daily life with others.

His relationship with family, ideas on the future.

Factors of his background that may have a bearing on learning.

Conflicts or concerns, especially those of an unconscious nature, which may be disturbing.

Skills, talents, abilities and interests which can be encouraged.

Meaning of placement to the child and family—its bearing.

How the child has learned to get along, to protect himself, to assert himself.

Steps we may take:

Show the youngster our interest, our willingness to reach out to him when he is ready, our acceptance and understanding of him.

Show him that we feel confident in our ability to live with him.

Show optimism in his ability to change and improve.

Encourage, through the institution program, special classes and study opportunities based on a child's needs and level of performance.

Encourage other children to support those who try even though they cannot always achieve heights. Show acceptance; others will follow.

Seek out interests on which a child can build and find some success.

Encourage caseworker and administrative staff to clarify family factors which may be causing some problem for the child, to find help for the child in resolving more basic conflicts and problems and in easing tensions.

Support efforts aimed at getting the interest and cooperation of family members to encourage the child in school work and to help child face realistic goals.

Offer credit or reward for effort, for trying or for some improvement, rather than for specific grades and honor rolls.

Visit the school and teacher to show interest and support for child.

Vary the degree of study-time supervision according to the needs of individuals.

Offer special individual help when beneficial and practical.

Seek an understanding with the teacher concerning study demands and expectations. Agree on the amount of pressure to be put on the child.

Consult with caseworker or administrator regarding factors which may bear on a child's performance.

Seek the help of another child for the slow learner when this is of mutual benefit.

With some children firm handling may be best, such as depriving them of some free time and assigning special studies. They may be looking for limits and for the houseparent to set expectations.

VII. Extra Sessions

25. WHAT QUESTIONS NEED ANSWERING?

The success or failure of a houseparent may be determined to a degree by the help and training that she receives upon her arrival and during the early months on the job. Although personality and talent and skill are important, the special nature of this type of work requires consistent and regular assistance, support, guidance, and training in carrying out the responsibility.

What questions should a houseparent raise as a new staff member?

What are my responsibilities—especially those which will involve my more immediate attention?

What are the most important rules which will confront me right away? These might include rules pertaining to:

Clothing	Sunday
Laundry	Visitors
Daily routine	Permissions
Supplies	Recreation
Church	Off-campus activity
School	Dating
Food	

Children are concerned about what the new staff member will do. They may deliberately test out the person in order to get a quick sense of what the approach is. Without pretending to know all, the new staff member, by having some information, can avoid some pitfalls and uncertainty.

Briefly, what is the institution attempting to do? What are its aims and goals?

Who are the children with whom I will live? A brief thumbnail sketch of each one can be helpful.

Who are the adults with whom I will live? This would include those who have the most immediate contact with the new person.

What other persons will have dealings with the boys or girls under my care? What are their responsibilities and how do mine interact with theirs?

How will they—children and adults—most likely react to me as a newcomer? (It may be reassuring to the new staff member to know this.)

What might be my best beginning approach?

How can I discipline and set limits?

What are some things I might do with the children during these early days on the job? How can I become better acquainted with them?

What's different about this work from what I have done before? *To whom* can I go for help and *when* and *with what*?

When can I do my personal business and pursue my other interests?

Most of the above information and guidance should come through discussions with the staff member who will take on supervision of the new person. Some of it may be helpful in written form.

New staff members need help in making the first adjustments to persons and activities with whom and with which they will have contact. They do not need to be loaded down with every scrap of information and hearsay. Their help should come in a planned way from persons who have a stake in supervision. In this way, they will form their trust and confidence with the person who must consistently carry through with them in their work. By being forced to lean in the direction of other persons doing the same job, the new workers may get wrong impressions and directions and may lose a working relationship with their supervisors that may be vital.

In most new situations, a person does not begin to feel a part until he has found acceptance by other members and by the leaders of the group, and feels that he has come out of his own conviction and desire. The new houseparent is unlikely to be effective until she finds acceptance by other staff members and by the people in charge and recognizes that she wants to be here and do this work.

What questions should a houseparent raise as a more settled staff member?

What situation has brought each child in my group to this place? What are his specific problems? What has caused them? What experiences or influences are part of his life? What are our goals and planning for him?

What family members are active and how am I to respond to them and about them?

What should each child gain from me? What are the unique responsibilities that are mine? What is the true nature of my job?

How do children grow normally? What are some of the reasons that children do not develop normally in all areas?

How do I work best with other staff in the interests of boys and girls? What are the responsibilities of other staff and their importance to the program?

What are some of the serious problems of people and how might I understand them better? This will be basic to understanding the family circumstances.

How should I handle special difficulties of children, such as bed wetting, stealing, thumb sucking, tantrums?

What part does my own personality play in this work? How should I understand and discipline myself?

What are the purposes of the institution program? What is meant by group-care? What are its strengths and weaknesses?

What happens to children in groups? How can I effectively work with groups?

What else is being done in the child welfare field? How do other people and agencies work?

These are among the important questions that require answers for the houseparent who has overcome the first hurdles and settles down to this as her career. Many of these questions only have real meaning after the person has had some practical experience. The answers may come through:

Supervisory conferences on a regular basis.
Direct support and help from the director.
Staff meetings around everyday problems.
Case conferences around needs of individual children.
Special institutes and conferences.
Reading materials.
Personal thought, study, and reflection.

Houseparents must carry heavy responsibility themselves but should not ever become so independent that they do not feel ready to learn. They cannot stand alone, for if they do, children will suffer. There are reasons why children need the rest of the staff, the program, and the community, and therefore the houseparent must learn to fit herself and cottage into this network.

26. SUBSTITUTING FOR THE REGULAR HOUSEPARENT

The person who assumes the care of a group of children in a cottage or dormitory becomes a very important person in the lives of these young people and in the conduct of the cottage program. Although she does not become related to each child in the sense of a real parent, she comes to represent care and security and protection and love. The regular houseparent, although not through any easy process, develops with the children a pattern of living which continues in the cottage even as children may move along to other groups.

It is not possible or good that a houseparent should so completely devote herself to a cottage group that nothing else is of interest or of importance to her. It is difficult to strike a middle ground between sufficient interest and dedication to the cottage program, and too much interest and dedication. The cottage itself must remain as integral part of the program of the total institution. The houseparent must remain an integral part of the staff. Children should not be led into such close relationships with a houseparent that they cannot move along to a better or necessary placement or that they cannot work out, constructively, their relationships with other adult people. The houseparent needs to be refreshed by other interests and contacts, apart from the institution. In order to help children grow and develop in today's world, she needs to keep related to that world herself and be a part of it. Children need change, too, even from someone they like. If this is not too upsetting and disorganized, the change will be helpful to them.

Most child-caring institutions or centers have found the necessity, and also the wisdom of providing substitute houseparents who take over for the regular houseparent, enabling her to have time off from her responsibilities. Arrangements vary greatly as to the amount of time off and the responsibility placed in the hands of the substitute, or relief, or supply, houseparent. Most places schedule regular time off, which includes over-night arrangements. In some institutions, more than one person may be assigned to a unit, with one having cooking responsibilities. On days off, the remaining staff person carries the full responsibility. The most usual arrangement is for certain persons to be designated as substitute houseparents and to rotate from group to group providing this service.

Values of a substitute arrangement:

Relieves regular houseparent so she can pursue her own interests and rest.

Provides cottage children with experiences with a different adult, with change even though in a small degree, with a break in monotony.

Reminds children that even a change in houseparent will not mean a loss of placement, of security, and of care.

Helps develop additional staff strength. Helps the over-all program.

Brings the cottage into focus as a part of the total operation.

Complications which can arise:

Some children may respond sharply to a change of any kind and may thus disrupt the rest of the group.

Too much variance between the approach of the substitute and the regular houseparent, thus creating upset for group and also staff.

Too little communication between the two so that there is no carry-over.

Too much communication so that one feels responsible for the other's actions. Too much reporting of incidents.

Things do not usually run as smoothly during the substitute's days. Housekeeping slips.

The substitute houseparent does not have the opportunity to follow-through on training, guidance, or discipline matters.

The substitute houseparent cannot settle down to any group and must move about and make an adjustment each time.

Either may find it hard to relinquish close relationship to certain children or may be concerned as to what will happen when some children are left in the care of the other.

The problem of sharing of bedroom space.

The regular houseparent may not thoroughly relinquish responsibility to the substitute and may reappear during her time off or try to control by admonitions as she leaves.

Differences between regular and substitute work:

The substitute houseparent has more chance to know the institution, different staff, and different children.

The regular houseparent has continuing planning responsibilities, such as for clothing, dating, budgeting, school supplies, vacations and visits.

The regular houseparent has more opportunity to carry out a method and to follow through on action.

The regular houseparent feels more at home in the cottage, more able to change furnishings and has an understanding of the routine and reasons for it.

Children understand that the regular houseparent has greater say-so and responsibility.

The substitute houseparent is away from her own private room and many of her own personal belongings.

The regular houseparent works more intensively with the children, knows them better and works more closely with the casework staff and the teachers.

Steps toward a smoother substitute plan:

Through discussions, such as in staff meetings, arrive at a clear understanding of the role of the substitute houseparent.

Make it essential for the regular houseparent to separate from the cottage group during time off.

Set up a system of supervision so that the substitute will look to a supervisor, other than the regular houseparent, for help and guidance.

Occasionally, arrange for joint conferences between the regular and substitute houseparents together with the supervisor.

Set up a plan whereby each person is informed of important events which have developed during time off.

Have regular houseparent indicate clearly what the routine of the cottage may be and the commitments of children for the period when she will be off.

Have regular houseparent prepare children for her going away and for the time of return, explaining who the substitute will be, if there is any question of this.

Be clear about the responsibility of the substitute for what has happened during the time the regular staff person has been on duty.

Be clear about what leeway the substitute houseparent has during her period with a group.

The substitute houseparent should plan to do some special things with youngsters during her time on. This may, for best results, be talked over with the regular houseparent. The substitute may bring a few of her own supplies.

Plan for substitute to be with a group for sufficient time to make it possible for her to build a relationship and to develop a pattern for working with a group.

Consider the best possible time of the day for a substitute to take over, so the transition will work out most smoothly.

If possible, provide the substitute houseparent with a special room for use during her time on duty, so that she does not have to use the regular houseparent's bedroom.

Interrelatedness. The regular and the substitute houseparents are not in competition with one another. They may work in different ways. What they accomplish may be different. The substitute's time in a cottage should not be regarded as just a stop-gap measure or just a holding action. She has a definite contribution to make, which will vary from that of the regular houseparent. Yet, these two staff members must, in a general way, work together so that children sense a spirit of unity. As in any substituting arrangement, whether it be in a private home, in an office, in a church, in a factory, there will be differences and frictions developing. A staff has to accept the differences and try to work them out so that children will gain from the plan.